Cambridge Elements

Elements in the Philosophy of Martin Heidegger
edited by
Filippo Casati
Lehigh University
Daniel O. Dahlstrom
Boston University

HEIDEGGER AND THE ELEMENTS OF (HUMAN) BEING

S. Montgomery Ewegen
Trinity College, Connecticut

Shaftesbury Road, Cambridge CB2 8EA, United Kingdom

One Liberty Plaza, 20th Floor, New York, NY 10006, USA

477 Williamstown Road, Port Melbourne, VIC 3207, Australia

314–321, 3rd Floor, Plot 3, Splendor Forum, Jasola District Centre,
New Delhi – 110025, India

103 Penang Road, #05–06/07, Visioncrest Commercial, Singapore 238467

Cambridge University Press is part of Cambridge University Press & Assessment,
a department of the University of Cambridge.

We share the University's mission to contribute to society through the pursuit of
education, learning and research at the highest international levels of excellence.

www.cambridge.org
Information on this title: www.cambridge.org/9781009647953
DOI: 10.1017/9781009647915

© S. Montgomery Ewegen 2025

This publication is in copyright. Subject to statutory exception and to the provisions of relevant collective licensing agreements, no reproduction of any part may take place without the written permission of Cambridge University Press & Assessment.

When citing this work, please include a reference to the DOI 10.1017/9781009647915

First published 2025

A catalogue record for this publication is available from the British Library

ISBN 978-1-009-64795-3 Hardback
ISBN 978-1-009-64793-9 Paperback
ISSN 2976-5668 (online)
ISSN 2976-565X (print)

Cambridge University Press & Assessment has no responsibility for the persistence or accuracy of URLs for external or third-party internet websites referred to in this publication and does not guarantee that any content on such websites is, or will remain, accurate or appropriate.

Heidegger and the Elements of (Human) Being

Elements in the Philosophy of Martin Heidegger

DOI: 10.1017/9781009647915
First published online: March 2025

S. Montgomery Ewegen
Trinity College, Connecticut
Author for correspondence: S. Montgomery Ewegen, shane.ewegen@trincoll.edu

Abstract: By way of an analysis of Heidegger's use of the elements of earth, water, air, and fire as a means to describe the unfolding of being, this Element offers a novel account of Heidegger's understanding of the human. By covering a variety of texts from the late 1920s through the early 1950s (including several of his recently published Black Notebooks), this Element demonstrates the manner in which these elements comprise, for Heidegger, the very being of the human.

Keywords: elementality, fire, air, water, earth

© S. Montgomery Ewegen 2025

ISBNs: 9781009647953 (HB), 9781009647939 (PB), 9781009647915 (OC)
ISSNs: 2976-5668 (online), 2976-565X (print)

Contents

	Introduction	1
1	Earth: The Protector	5
2	Water: The Sole Catastrophe	19
3	Air: The Sign	33
4	Fire: The Sufferer	47
	Conclusion: The Shepherd	56
	References	59

Introduction

What is, for Heidegger, the proper *element* of the human? Even a reader who has spent very little time with Heidegger's work will anticipate straightaway the answer to this question. Given the origins and path of Heidegger's thought, and given the questions that preoccupied him along that path, there is only one possible answer to the above question: *being*. Heidegger himself states this clearly enough in his "Letter on Humanism" from 1946:

> If the name "ethics," in keeping with the basic meaning of the word *ethos*, should now say that "ethics" ponders the abode of the human, then that thinking which thinks the truth of being as the inceptual element of the human [*das anfängliche Element des Menschen*], as one who ek-sists, is in itself the original ethics.[1]

The truth of being is the inceptual element of the human, the abode (*Aufenthalt*) in which the human fundamentally dwells: it is the most basic, foundational, and archaic element to which the human owes its essence. As the abode, the *Aufenthalt*, of the human, being is where the human *stays* and is *held*, that of which it is most fundamentally *comprised*.[2] Being *keeps* and *contains* the human, *composes* and *encompasses* it, serving as the most primitive and primordial element in which and in relation to which the human carries out its earthly sojourn.[3]

But what, for Heidegger, "is" *being*? The relatively short word limit of the present Element almost forbids the posing of this question – for, again, even a reader who has spent very little time with Heidegger's work will know that it was that question most of all that animated his thinking through the course of his long career.[4] Throughout his vast corpus, Heidegger posed the question of the meaning of being again and again, almost *obsessively*, though the manner of that posing, and the vocabulary and conceptual tools by which it was carried out, changed over time. To even *begin* to offer a survey of Heidegger's long arch of thinking regarding the question of the meaning of being would be impossible within the constraints of the current Element – or, perhaps, within *any* single project.

That being said, it is safe to say that, from at least the 1930s on, Heidegger understood being as the emerging clearing in/as which beings open up phenomenally: it is, so to speak, phenomenality itself.[5] Whether he casts it in terms of "unconcealment," "the clearing," "the event of appropriation," the "worlding of the world," the "fouring of the fourfold," or one of his many other formulations,

---

[1] GA 9: 356/258.
[2] All of these italicized words are possible translations of the German *Aufenthalt*.
[3] On *Aufenthalt*, see Bambach 2021, 685–689.   [4] See GA 94: 22/17.
[5] See Richardson 2003, 6.

Heidegger thinks of being in the direction of the eventuating clearing of a space-time in which, and in some sense *as* which, the human – and, properly speaking, *only* the human – dwells. Being is the expanse, the medium, the *dimension* in which beings may be and in which the human stands in a unique and privileged manner.[6] It is the primordial or inceptual element from out of which the essence of the human is determined, the very clearing and opening of a possible existential abode for human being.

Precisely owing to the manner in which being serves as this primordial element, the question of the meaning of being is inextricably tied up with the question of the meaning of the *human*: for it is *only* the human, according to Heidegger, who stands in a *questioning* relation to being.[7] As Heidegger indicates again and again, though never with static rigidity, being and the human are co-implicated, intimately and mutually dependent, *intertwined*. The human is the counterpart, the counter*word*, to being:[8] being *needs* the human in order to show itself in its proper aspect; the human, for its part, needs being in order to be what it most properly is.[9] This intertwinement of being and the human is captured in Heidegger's language, in the previously cited passage, of the *elemental* character of the truth of being. The human is *immersed* in being, *surrounded* by it, *rooted* in it, so much so that it is at times difficult to tell where the one ends and the other begins, and this means that, when one attempts to think being, one is also thereby compelled to think the human, as well as the relation – if indeed it *is* a "relation" – between the two.[10]

In his efforts to think through this intimate relationship between the human and being, Heidegger employs a vast vocabularic arsenal over the decades. This arsenal includes words like *Dasein* ("the *there* of being"), *Daseyn*, *die Sterbliche* ("the mortal"), and, of course, *Mensch* ("human"); it also includes more grandiloquent expressions such as "The Shepherd of Being," "The Protector of Being," "The Gatherer," "The Questioner," "The Ones to Come," and so on. The size of this arsenal increases twofold if one takes into account Heidegger's penchant for using hyphens as a deconstructive tool, a practice that yields such terms as *Da-sein*, *Da-seyn*, and so forth. If one also pays heed to Heidegger's occasional (and philosophically critical) practice of crossing out certain of these terms – D̶a̶s̶e̶i̶n̶, D̶a̶s̶e̶y̶n̶, etcetera – then one begins to appreciate just how rich and varied Heidegger's lexicon was for describing the single being which, after all, we ourselves always already are, a being whose very being is determined principally and essentially through its relation to being.

---

[6] GA 9: 334/254.   [7] See GA 40: 3/4.   [8] See GA 71: 290/251.
[9] See, for example, GA 40: 64/92; GA 6.2: 441/76; GA 99: 126.   [10] See GA 99: 151.

Such a variety of vocabulary points to the *restlessness* and *insatiableness* with which Heidegger approached the question of the human, and to the *inadequacy* of any single term, or any level of discourse (i.e., ontic, ontological, poetic, inceptual, etc.), to capture every element of that being. It also demonstrates that Heidegger's engagement with this question was always *on the way*, that it never came to a standstill or a stop, that it never reached a definitive end. It is for this reason that one finds, even in Heidegger's final texts, the posing of the *question* of the human and an experimenting with finding the most suitable vocabulary to capture its true essential character.

Because of the richness and expansiveness of the path of Heidegger's thinking, there are innumerable ways one could go about structuring a compendium of his understanding of the human. For example, one could proceed chronologically with the hope of offering a historical survey of the development of Heidegger's terminology and concomitant understanding of the human, beginning with *Dasein* (in *Being and Time*), turning to *Daseyn* (in, e.g., *The Event*), and ending with "the mortal" (in, e.g., the Bremen lectures). Or one could focus entirely on the aforementioned grander expressions, measuring the particular meanings of each and comparing the contexts out of which they arise. Or one could simply trace Heidegger's use of the term "human" (*Mensch*) over the decades, showing how it accrues or sheds different nuances and valences as Heidegger's thinking develops. Each of these paths would doubtlessly yield fruitful results, although each carries within itself its own set of silent preconceptions and interpretive biases, as would be the case with any path that one chose (including the present one).

In what follows, a somewhat more oblique path will be taken into Heidegger's thinking of the human. Partly in deference to the title and style of the series in which this Element appears, but above all because of Heidegger's language regarding the *elementality* of being, the present Element will trace Heidegger's understanding of the human along the axis of the so-called classical elements: earth, water, air, and fire. The guiding thesis of the present project is that these elements serve as a particularly fruitful path by means of which to survey Heidegger's (re)consideration of the human. As will come to light, these elements figure significantly into various of Heidegger's texts throughout his long career of thinking, all the way from *Being and Time* (1927) up through the 1950s. One can thus traverse nearly the chronological entirety of Heidegger's thought by means of the passages in which these elements appear, tracking the contours of his understanding of the human in terms of their specific valences. Simply put, earth, water, air, and fire all show up at various points throughout Heidegger's corpus and provide him with another way of articulating the structure and sojourn of the human, of accounting for what it *means* to be the sole being that *stands* in a relation to being.

As Section 1 demonstrates, the element of *earth* plays a significant role in Heidegger's understanding of the human. Orienting itself around the "Myth of Cura" from *Being and Time*, this section argues that earth, which comes to play so prominent a role in Heidegger's middle and late periods, already serves a foundational (albeit somewhat different) role in his first major work. As the element out of which *things* (broadly conceived) are made, earth is omnipresent in the human's experience of its world; moreover, as the concealed ground upon which the clearing of the world depends, earth is that without which the human could not experience its role as the *there* of being's unfolding (i.e., as the *Da* of *Sein*).

Section 2 explores the foundational role that *water* plays within Heidegger's configuration of the human. By first focusing on Heidegger's lectures on Hölderlin's river poetry from the 1930s, water is seen to play an elemental role in human *dwelling* – that is, the manner by which the human comes to occupy its proper place. By bringing these lectures into conversation with the "Letter on Humanism," Heidegger's fundamentally *hydroponic* understanding of language, as the manifold unfolding of meaningfulness, is brought to light. For Heidegger, the human is that entity who is *immersed* in language, who *swims* in it, in very much the same way that a fish lives immersed in water.

Section 3 focuses on the extent to which *air* figures into Heidegger's lectures on Heraclitus from 1943–1944, the Bremen lectures from 1949, and *What Is Called Thinking* from 1951–1952. Playing a role both in Heidegger's understanding of the clearing of being and that of the human ψυχή, air is seen to be the *atmosphere* of thinking into which the human must enter in order to find its proper abode. Ultimately, the human is presented as the sole entity capable of being drawn into the *draft* of being, of drawing such a draft into itself, and of thereby breathing the atmosphere of being.

Section 4 explores Heidegger's use of *fire* as a means by which to understand the human's role in the clearing of being. Orienting itself around Heidegger's reinscription of the ancient myth of Prometheus, this section charts the parameters of a conflict which, for Heidegger, characterizes the experience of the contemporary human, namely the conflict between the *artificial* fires of technicity and the *primordial* fires of the inception of being. For Heidegger, the human must turn away from the former and toward the latter in order to enter into its ownmost essence. It is further suggested that Heidegger's thinking of the human remains fundamentally Promethean insofar as the human is depicted as an entity whose ultimate fate and function is *to suffer* the fire of being.

Each section thus traces the manner in which Heidegger uses the language of the classical elements to bring the structure of human being, and the nature of its relation to being, into greater clarity. (As will be seen, such language is *never* metaphorical for Heidegger, but is rather *phenomenological* in a robust sense.) Moreover, while exploring texts from throughout Heidegger's corpus, each section also attempts to tie each element back into Heidegger's understanding of *Dasein* as it is presented in *Being and Time*, and specifically into the "Myth of Cura" recounted therein. It is thus suggested that these elements played a crucial role in Heidegger's understanding of the human from at least 1927 on.

In sum, the present Element will show that the *project* of being human, for Heidegger, entails coming into a greater awareness of the elemental character of being and the role that earth, water, air, and fire play in its unfolding. Simply put, to be human – or rather to first *become* human in the fullest, most authentic sense – one must first come to grasp the truth of being in its full elementality.

1 Earth: The Protector

The human, so the story goes, is *earth-made*. This story appears quite nearly at the end of Division One of *Being and Time*, after dozens of pages of dense and highly technical exploration of the structure of human being. This story – this *myth* or *fable* (*Fabel*) – hails from the Latin author Gaius Julius Hyginus, though it made its way to Heidegger by way of Herder, Goethe, and K. Burdach.[11] In a move that has perplexed readers of *Being and Time* since its appearance, Heidegger turns to this fable as a way to confirm and authorize his preceding analysis of the human, claiming that the myth serves as a pretheoretical, and therefore *more originary and authentic*, articulation of that being, insisting that the story "should make plain that our existential interpretation is not a mere fabrication, but that as an ontological 'construction' it is well grounded [*Boden*] and has been sketched out beforehand in *elemental* [*elementaren*] ways."[12] The myth – the so-called Myth of Cura, as quoted by Heidegger – is as follows:

> Once when "Care" was crossing a river, she saw some clay [*Erdreich*]; she thoughtfully took a piece and began to shape it. While she was thinking about what she had made, Jupiter came by. "Care" asked him to give it spirit, and this he gladly granted. But when she wanted her name to be bestowed upon it, Jupiter forbade this and demanded that it be given his name instead. While "Care" and Jupiter were arguing, Earth (Tellus) arose, and desired that her name be conferred on the creature, since she had offered it part of her body.

---

[11] GA 2: 262/242.
[12] GA 2: 262/242; my emphasis. See also GA 20: 418/302: "Such interpretations have the primary advantage of being drawn from an originally naive view of *Dasein* itself and so of playing a particularly positive role for all interpretation."

They asked Saturn to be the judge. And Saturn gave them the following decision, which seemed to be just: "Since you, Jupiter, have given its spirit, you shall receive that spirit at death; and since you, Earth, have given its body, you shall receive its body. But since 'Care' first shaped this creature, she shall possess it as long as it lives. And because there is a dispute among you as to its name, let it be called '*homo*,' for it is made out of *humus* (earth)."[13]

According to this story – a story upon which Heidegger, in a certain sense, bases the entire weight of his existential analytic, letting it serve as the authorization and guarantee of the analyses therein[14] – the human is composed of earth and bears the mark of that composition in its very name: the human is *earth-made*, its name attesting to its intimacy with the earth. The story also states that *care* – which, in the pages immediately leading up to the myth, Heidegger has shown to be the very ground of the ontological structure of human being – is that which forms the human out of earth, that which is responsible for this earthy composition: it is as though *care* and *earth* were bound together in some intimate and indissoluble way, as if the sort of care that characterizes the core of human existence were itself characterized, or somehow forever intertwined with, the earth.

But what would such intertwinement look like? What is the nature of the relationship between *earth* and *care*? In order to begin to answer these questions, one must first come to greater clarity regarding the general character of the human itself as Heidegger conceives of it in *Being and Time*. The appellation with which Heidegger most often refers to this character is *Dasein*. A perfectly common word within the history of German philosophy and German discourse more broadly, *Dasein* most immediately refers to *existence* in the generic, nonphilosophical sense (i.e., the way that anything, from a cloud to a cat to a typewriter, could be said to exist). However, around 1924, Heidegger highjacked this word, so to speak, and began to ask of it a great deal – indeed, he began to ask of this word *almost* everything.[15] It is hardly hyperbolic to say that, at least for a time – and, in the end, the word itself proves to be all about *time*, insofar as it ultimately refers to the only entity who, according to Heidegger, experiences time[16] – Heidegger placed the entire edifice of his thinking upon the word *Dasein*, making it the very cornerstone of his thought. Bearing the weight of this great edifice, the little word *Dasein* became almost limitlessly rich in its

---

[13] GA 2: 262–263/184.
[14] Heidegger writes that the "demonstrative force [of the story] is 'merely historical,'" and yet it presents a "primordial expression" of the being of *Dasein* and has a "special weight" (GA 2: 261/241). On Heidegger's "ambivalent" attitude toward this myth, see Hyland 1997, especially 92–94.
[15] On Heidegger's innovation of this word, see Polt 1999, 29–30. [16] See GA 40: 64/92.

signification, and ultimately came to name the very aperture of being's unfolding and the human's relation to (or as) that aperture.

Etymologically, the term *Dasein* means "being-there," and it is this sense that guides Heidegger's analysis of the human as *Dasein* (both within *Being and Time* and far beyond it). As *Being and Time* argues, *Dasein* is principally that being whose being serves as the *there* (*Da*) – that is, the clearing opening – of being's unfolding.[17] Although the clearing/opening structure of *Dasein* will find greater emphasis in Heidegger's later works, already in *Being and Time Dasein* is said to be the site where being opens itself up and where (or in which) beings show themselves as such:

> When we talk in an ontically figurative way of the *lumen naturale* in the human, we have in mind nothing other than the existential-ontological structure of this entity, that it is in such a way as to be its "there." To say that it is "illuminated" means that as being-in-the-world it is cleared in itself, not through any other entity, but in such a way that it is itself the clearing.[18]

The human "is itself the clearing" of (its) being: it is the open in which beings show themselves as such. Although this appears to offer a straightforward identification between *Dasein* and the clearing (*die Lichtung*), Heidegger will clarify in later texts, such as the *Zollikon Seminars*, that the relationship between the human and the clearing is more complicated:

> The human being is the guardian of the clearing, of the disclosive appropriating Event [of being]. He is not the clearing himself, not the entire clearing, nor is he identical with the whole of the clearing as such. But as the one ecstatically "standing out" into the clearing, he himself is essentially cleared [*gelichtet*], and thus cleared himself in a distinguished way. Therefore, he is related to, belongs to, and is appropriated by the clearing. Da-sein's being needed as the shepherd of the clearing is a distinguished manner of belonging to the clearing.[19]

The human is the "shepherd" of the clearing, to the extent that it stands out in the open of that clearing, owes its own essence to it, and preserves and safeguards that clearing.

Such standing out within the open clearing of being – or, as he will often put it, the *truth* of being, where truth must be understood in the Greek sense of ἀλήθεια, or "unconcealment" – is what Heidegger calls "existence," and it is a foundational (and controversial) principle of his that human *Dasein*, and *only*

---

[17] See Richardson 2003, 20.   [18] GA 2: 177/125.
[19] GA 89: 223/178. The notion of the human as the guardian, shepherd, or watcher of being will dominant much of Heidegger's middle and late thought. See Keiling's (2021) succinct definition of the human in Heidegger in "Human Being," 402.

human *Dasein*, exists in the sense in which he employs the term. As Heidegger puts it at one point in *Being and Time*, "*Dasein* exists, and it alone. Thus existence is standing out and perduring the openness of the there."[20] Such existence is to be understood as the manner in which the human *relates* to the possibilities that present themselves to it (or, as we will later see, the manner in which it *cares* about such possibilities) within the clearing, the way that it can be – or, indeed, *has* to be, *has* to choose, one way or another[21] – these possibilities. Such possibilities *present* themselves from out of the specific, factical situation in which any given *Dasein* finds itself: to stand (in) the truth of the being – to be (in) the *there* of being's clearing – is to have been thrown into the present, from out of the past, and in such a way as to relate to one's (future) possibilities. It is this temporal unfolding, this interplay of past and future within a present, that characterizes the unique existence of the human (according to Heidegger): to be *Dasein* is to be the "there" both of the *where*, but also of the *when*, of being's unfolding. *Dasein* is the placing, the spacing, and the pacing of the opening of being.

As the entity who stands out in the clearing of being, the human has a certain pretheoretical understanding of, or immersion within, that clearing: that is to say, the human is *in the world* and has an average, everyday, operational *understanding* of being in terms of which it navigates that world. In each case, *Dasein* always finds itself *in* the world, not (only) in a spatial sense, but more primarily in the sense of *dwelling* and *abiding* in that world, of being *familiar* and *concerned* with the beings with which it always finds itself within the perimeters of that world. Regarding this manner of dwelling, Heidegger offers the following:

> "*In*" is derived from "*innan*" – "to reside," "*habitare*," "to dwell." "*An*" signifies "I am accustomed," "I am familiar with," "I look after something." It has the signification of "*colo*" in the senses of "*habito*" and "*diligo*." The entity to which being-in in this signification belongs is one which we have characterized as that entity which in each case I myself am [*bin*]. The expression "*bin*" is connected with "*bei*," and so "*ich bin*" ["I am"] means in its turn "I reside [*ich wohne*]" or "dwell alongside" the world, as that which is familiar to me in such and such a way.[22]

The manner of *Dasein*'s "being-in" is thus to be understood in terms of *dwelling*, of residing alongside other entities so as to be caught up with them, concerned with them. In his later *Building Dwelling Thinking* (from 1951), in a passage that almost mirrors the passage just cited from *Being and Time*,

---

[20] GA 2: 177/125. [21] See GA 2: 56/39. [22] GA 2: 73/51.

Heidegger goes into greater detail into this dwelling that characterizes the being of *Dasein*, and in such a way as to tie it explicitly to the *earth*:

> When we speak of dwelling we usually think of an activity that the human performs alongside many other activities. We work here and dwell there. We do not merely dwell – that would be virtual inactivity – we practice a profession, we do business, we travel and lodge on the way, now here, now there. *Bauen* originally means to dwell. Where the word *bauen* still speaks in its original sense it also says how far the nature of dwelling reaches. That is, *bauen, buan, bhu, beo* are our word *bin* in the versions: *ich bin*, I am, *du bist*, you are, the imperative form *bis*, be. What then does *ich bin* mean? The old word *bauen*, to which the *bin* belongs, answers: *ich bin, du bist* mean: I dwell, you dwell. The way in which you are and I am, the manner in which we humans *are* on the earth [*auf der Erde sind*], is *Buan*, dwelling. To be a human being means: *to be on the earth* as a mortal [*als Sterblicher auf der Erde sein*]. It means to dwell.[23]

Dwelling of the sort in which *Dasein* essentially and always engages – its manner of being-in-the-world, to which it attests when it utters the words "I am" – takes place on, and thus remains in some manner bound to, the earth.

Given the fact that, so long as *Dasein is*, it is *in the world*, one could say that the world is *Dasein*'s *element* – and, indeed, at one point during his discussion of the *mitsein* of *Dasein* (i.e., the manner in which *Dasein* always finds itself alongside other *Dasein*, intertwined with them and their concerns), Heidegger speaks of the world in exactly these terms:

> They [i.e., other *Dasein*] are encountered from the *world* in which Da-sein, heedful and circumspect, essentially dwells. ... This nearest and elemental [*elementare*] way of Da-sein of being encountered in the world goes so far that even one's *own* Da-sein *initially* becomes "discoverable" by *looking away* from its "experiences" and the "center of its actions" or by not yet "seeing" them all. Da-sein initially finds "itself" in *what* it does, needs, expects, has charge of, in the things at hand which it initially *takes care of* in the surrounding world.[24]

The world is that element of which the existence of *Dasein* most fundamentally consists and in terms of which it finds and orients itself, and this world, as seen above, is always a world *of the earth*, is always an *earthly* world.[25] In this way, the earth, along with the world, is elemental to *Dasein*'s being.

So long as it exists, *Dasein* finds itself *dispersed* within this element, cast forth within the *earthworld*; and so long as it finds itself in this earthworld, it

---

[23] GA 7: 149/147. [24] GA 2: 159/112.
[25] GA 96: 83/66: "The earth reposes on a ground into which it retracts its own mystery and, as something closed, protrudes out into a world."

finds itself amongst various other beings, engaged and concerned with them to varying extents. To be *Dasein* is *always* to find oneself in situations in which one is required, simply by virtue of existing, to engage with various "somethings," to always be, for example, "producing something, attending to something and looking after it, making use of something, giving something up and letting it go, undertaking, accomplishing, evincing, interrogating, considering, discussing, determining."[26] Each of these activities, and the limitless number of other such activities, is a mode or expression of the *concern* that characterizes the very being of *Dasein*, of the manner in which *Dasein cares* about (its) being.

Above all, this means that *Dasein* is such as to always find itself amongst *things*:[27] not "things" in the abstract – for one never walks into a room full of mere "things" – but *particular* things in their contextualized usefulness. In our day-to-day dealings, for example, we might encounter things "for writing, sewing, things for working, driving, measuring," etcetera.[28] Such things always stand in a network of relations to other things, each thing earning its particular character by way of the relation not only to the task at hand (i.e., the "in order to") for which it is employed, but also, and perhaps above all, through its relation to the other things to which it stands in proximity: "writing materials, pen, ink, paper, desk blotter, table, lamp, furniture, windows, doors, room."[29] Heidegger calls these things characterized by such contextualized usefulness "equipment," and it is *here*, with such equipment, that one can find further traces of the earth. The "things" that Heidegger has enumerated – inkstand, pen, ink, paper, blotting pad, table, lamp, furniture, window, doors, room – *all* hail from the earth. Indeed, *any and all things*, regardless of their function and material makeup, are made out of earth in the broadest sense: for there is no *thing* on earth that does not owe its material composition to the earth, even if that earthly origin is oftentimes difficult to see.[30] To this extent, *every* τέχνη, and *every* product produced by a τέχνη, relates to and deals with transmutations of the earth. One imagines Heidegger holding a wooden pen, filled with ink derived from vegetal sources, writing his incomprehensible words in his inscrutable penmanship onto the paper made from wood pulp, the wooden chair in which he sits creaking with the sound reminiscent of the swaying trees that were felled to

---

[26] GA 2: 76/83.

[27] Mitchell is doubtlessly correct to emphasize the chasm that stands between the "things" of *Being and Time* and the "things" of Heidegger's later thinking, the latter of which, of course, entail *earth* as an essential element (Mitchell 2015, 10–12). Nevertheless, earth, at least in a certain sense, can be seen to operate within Heidegger's analysis of "things" from *Being and Time*.

[28] GA 2: 92/64.   [29] GA 2: 92/64.

[30] The only exceptions to this include meteorites, moon rocks, space dust, and other extraterrestrial materials that have, either through natural process or human conquest, made their way to the earth. But none of these objects would qualify as "equipment" in a Heideggerian sense, at least not as matters currently stand.

make it. Even when the human today sits on a plastic chair typing away at a plastic keyboard while staring blearily into a glass screen, that human is *still* connected to the earth through touching and seeing, though such a connection is progressively more difficult to see, more difficult to feel. Nevertheless, through its interaction with the things around it, the human forever remains connected to the earth, even if that connection remains, for the most part, *concealed*.

As Heidegger gets deeper into his analysis of equipment, one sees the concealed role of the earth almost become explicit as he discusses the material makeup of certain equipment and how such material is characterized by a referential structure:

> A reference to "materials" is contained in the work at the same time. The work is dependent upon leather, thread, nails, and similar things. Leather in its turn is produced from hides. These hides are taken from animals which were bred and raised by others. We also find animals in the world which were not bred and raised and even when they have been raised these beings produce themselves in a certain sense. Thus beings are accessible in the surrounding world which in themselves do not need to be produced and are always already at hand. Hammer, tongs, nails in themselves refer to – they consist of – steel, iron, metal, stone, wood. "Nature" is also discovered in the use of useful things, "nature" in the light of products of nature.[31]

In other words, pieces of equipment refer to the material out of which they are made: steel, iron, metal, mineral, wood – *elements*, in other words, pulled from the earth, out of which the various instruments of our equipment are made.[32] As one deals with such equipment, engrossed in the task at hand and more or less unaware of the equipment itself depending on the level of one's engrossment, one would nevertheless remain in contact with the earthly origins of such equipment, one's hands cradling the earth while being entirely unaware of it.[33] Simply put, every *thing* points to, and ultimately derives from, the earth.

Thus, in its dealings with equipment, the human is continually, ineradicably in contact with the earth. As that being in the world who always finds itself amidst things (in the earlier clarified sense of equipment), the human forever finds itself *on* the earth surrounded by things *of* the earth. Any time that the human relates itself to things – which is, quite literally, *all* of the time – it relates itself to what comes from the earth, and thus to the earth in at least this fundamental sense. Even that human who walks along a concrete walkway in a big city where any sign of the "natural world" has been replaced with a "man-made" edifice: even this human remains in contact with the earth, to the extent that *all* equipment refers, one way or another, to the earth from which its most

---

[31] GA 2: 94/66. On this, see Polt 1999, 51.   [32] Compare Biemel and Emad 1980, 56.
[33] See GA 5: 19/160.

basic elements originated. The world of the human, in whatever configuration it takes, remains *earthmade*.

One can see further traces of such contact with the earth in Heidegger's analysis of how the human, as *Dasein*, navigates its existential space.[34] Prior to any theoretical or mathematical representation of space and the objects within it (in terms, e.g., of Cartesian coordinates), *Dasein* relates itself to the things of its concern, bringing those things into the ambit of its care (i.e., into "nearness"), even while those things remain at some spatial distance. (E.g., one can think about the dinner waiting for one at home, thus bringing the concern for such dinner into the foreground of one's thoughts without actually bringing the dinner itself into physical proximity.) About such bringing-into-proximity – what Heidegger calls "de-distancing" (*Entfernen*) – he offers the following:

> De-distancing does not necessarily imply any explicit estimation of the farness of things at hand in relation to Da-sein. Above all, remoteness is never understood as measurable distance. If farness is estimated, this is done relative to the de-distancing in which everyday Da-sein is involved. In the calculative sense these estimations may be imprecise and variable, but they have their *own* thoroughly intelligible *definiteness* in the everydayness of Da-sein. We say that to go over there is a good walk, a stone's throw, as long as it takes to smoke a pipe.[35]

Heidegger's point is that, prior to any theoretical or mathematical projection of measurable distance, *Dasein* itself measures its distances in terms of its everyday experiences and projected possibilities. But: Can one not hear the silent call of the earth here, just below the surface, in these everyday expressions of distance? Would a *walk*, a *stone*, and a *pipe*, as "units" of spatial measurement, not carry within themselves references to the earth? Can one go for a walk, hold a stone in one's hand, or smoke tobacco in a way that loses connection to the earth? Wouldn't such expressions, even once they had passed over into the metaphorical, still bear some trace of that connection? And wouldn't *Dasein*, in making use of those expressions, bear witness in those moments to its ineradicable connection to the earth?

It light of all of this, one might wonder if the very appellation "*Dasein*," so important to Heidegger's reconsideration of the human, itself bears vague, diluted traces of this ineradicable connection to the earth. There are two ways in which this might be the case. First, the very sense of "thereness," as serving as the locative indicator of something, perhaps carries with itself an ineluctable reference of the earth. "Thereness" derives its meaning from an indicative *pointing*, a directional intimating that positions some ontic thing relative to

---

[34] We will return to the issue of *space* in Section 3. [35] GA 2: 141/98.

some other ontic thing. (e.g., "Where is the bathroom? Over *there*.") Insofar as every "there," at least initially and for the most part, takes place upon the *earth*, within the arena of *Dasein*'s earthly sojourn, one might well wonder whether the *Da* of *Dasein*, the *there* of being's unfolding, is in this way essentially connected to the earth: for it is only with the greatest abstraction that one could ever speak of any *there* in such a way as to sever its connection to the earth.[36]

Second, and less speculatively, the *Da*, at least for Heidegger's later thought, is often brought into explicit connection to the earth. During the 1930s and beyond, Heidegger emphasizes again and again that the clearing of being stands in intimate relation to the concealment characterized by earth, and that the former is only possible through its intimate connection to the latter. First developing this through his engagements with Hölderlin's poetry, then concretizing and radicalizing it in his "The Origin of the Work of Art" (1935–1936) and his subsequent work in the 1940s on the fourfold, earth comes to be seen as the essential, originary counterpart to world. For the purposes of the present section, what is most important in this connection is the way in which world is seen to be impossible *without* earth, and that it (thus) carries earth along with itself, so to speak, in its unfolding.[37] Heidegger suggests as much when he writes, in his *History of Beyng* (1938–1940), that "every world opens itself and remains configured to an earth,"[38] or even more forcefully when he writes that "the eventful appropriating of the There through the voice of silence, as clearing, at the same time lets earth find its way to world, the world to the human, the human to the god, and the god to the earth."[39] This formulation in particular indicates the indissoluble connection between world and earth, their mutual dependence and ineradicable intertwinement (along with the other poles of the fourfold). Moreover, it indicates that, insofar as the *Da* of *Dasein* is understood as bespeaking the opening of world, the human, grasped as *Dasein*, would always carry the earth along with itself through the clearing operations of its very being. As the one who is the *there* of being, the human, *worlding*, would do so *only on the basis* of the earth to which it remains essentially connected. Simply put, *Dasein* would have no world – it itself would not *be* a world – were it not for (the) earth.

When one turns back to *Being and Time* in the wake of Heidegger's later thinking concerning the relation of earth and world, one must be mindful of this omnipresent, albeit concealed, relation of world to earth, of earth to *Dasein*. One imagines Heidegger himself, rereading *Being and Time* years after its publication and adding his annotations. Such annotations come from a later point in

---

[36] One thinks, perhaps, of the reassuring expression "there, there," which seemingly has lost any and all connection to the earth.
[37] See Gadamer 1994, 190. [38] GA 69: 108/91. [39] GA 69: 126/107.

Heidegger's thinking, a thinking that, after *Being and Time*, had thought through Hölderlin, had written *Contributions to Philosophy*, *Mindfulness*, "The Origin of the Work of Art," "The Thing," etcetera, *all* of which address, to varying extents and in different ways, the earth and its role in the world of *Dasein*. One wonders if Heidegger, as he reread his analytic of *Dasein*, understood the *Da* therein as naming the earth, as pointing to it without ever drawing it completely to the fore, letting it remain where it rightfully belongs, namely as the *concealed* ground of the open clearing of being. One wonders if the "Myth of Cura," which expressly ties earth and care so intimately together, says precisely this.

In any case, one thing is certain: Heidegger does *not* talk about the earth in *Being and Time* in any overt detail. Despite the role that earth occupies therein, as elucidated above, earth remains an undeveloped theme and plays a merely implicit role within the text. It is almost as though early Heidegger *forgot* about the earth as he got caught up in thinking the world. Indeed, it is almost as if *Being and Time* itself were emblematic of the forgetting of the earth that Heidegger will later claim as being so characteristic of the contemporary age. For later Heidegger, the forgetting of earth is tantamount to – or, rather, part and parcel of – the forgetting of being that has beset the human within the current epoch. Such forgetting of being, and such forgetting of earth understood as the concealed ground of the emerging/clearing of being, is responsible for the destitution of the modern historical moment and the widespread destruction of the earth: for metaphysics, which is nothing other than the forgetfulness of being, has culminated in a situation where the earth itself has become little more than an object of *use*.[40] The human, whose very name, as we saw above, attests to that entity's bondage to earth, has forgotten the earth and through such forgetting has transformed it into an infinitely orderable and manipulatable unit of standing-reserve; and though such forgetting is not entirely the fault of the human, as it follows upon the self-withdrawing character of being itself, the human is nonetheless the site or the mechanism through which such devastation is carried out:

> Earth – ever since the planet has been conquered as "globe," the essential danger threatening the earth, namely, that its essence be simply denied, has risen to the highest pitch; for in every respect metaphysics (i.e., the forgettability of the setting-apart) aids in the misinterpretation of the essence of the earth.[41]

Earthmade, but forgetful of the earth, the human, whose very ontological core consists of care, walks carelessly upon the earth.

---

[40] See, for example, GA 9: 257/197; GA 71: 103/85; GA 96: 270/214.   [41] GA 99: 32.

The task for the human, then, would be to *remember* being, and it was charting the perimeters of that task that occupied pride of place within Heidegger's thinking from at least *Being and Time* on. By the mid 1930s, such remembering of being expressly entails the remembering of the concealing that belongs to being, the submerging that serves as the counterpoint to being's emerging. To the extent that earth names this concealing/submerging withdrawal that belongs to being, the project of remembering *being* plays out as a project of remembering the *earth*. One sees this, for example, in one of Heidegger's Black Notebooks (1938–1939), when Heidegger writes that

> historically – i.e., as bearing future humanity – the earth can come to be only if humans are previously thrust into the truth of beyng and if, on the basis of a disclosive thinking of beyng, the gods and humans themselves enter into the site of the battle over their destinies, from which battle the world first flashes up and the earth regains its obscurity.[42]

Remembering being – being "thrust" into it – the human would come to know the earth as the ground of the clearing's unfolding. Heidegger articulates this even more strongly in a later passage:

> But here is the origin of beings – i.e., of the fact that the world opens up and the earth is closed and each thing comes to stand in the clearing – provided the human being is able, as that encountering one, to be the "there" and from the spatiotemporal field of this "there" to see the structure of beings and to become the steward of the clearing which remains as long as it refuses itself, i.e., as long as its abyss compels into the plight of the grounding and denies to the human being, as the one assigned to beyng, every comfort in his own fabrications and thus bestows on him the height of his essence which finds itself in its beginning as it is appropriated by beyng itself.[43]

The remembering of earth depends upon the human *becoming* the "there," the *Da*, of being's unfolding, of *entering into* its proper role as *Da-sein*: in this way, the earth needs the human as much as the human needs the earth.

All of this draws our attention to a crucial aspect of Heidegger's understanding of the human as it develops after *Being and Time*, namely that the human is *not yet Dasein*.[44] Heidegger marks this "not-yet" character often in one of his Black Notebooks, where he writes, for example, that the human must be "placed *back* into *Dasein*," that it must follow "a great lone path" *into Dasein*,

---

[42] GA 95: 73/56. See also GA 95: 47/36: "Perhaps quite other modes and powers of the most intimate affiliation must awaken first and seek their track, if the human being is to find his way to *Dasein* and beyng is to become the hearth fire between earth and world. We turn aside all too readily into the customary, whose customariness we then mask from ourselves with the help of a worn-out ideal."
[43] GA 95: 304/237.   [44] See Polt 2006, 10, 215.

"liberating" itself for *Dasein* and "gathering" itself into it.[45] Heidegger expresses this in greater detail in his *Contributions to Philosophy* (1936–1938):

> Da-sein and human being are essentially related, inasmuch as Da-sein signifies the ground of the possibility of future human being, and humans are futural by accepting to be the "there," provided they understand themselves as the stewards of the truth of beyng. This stewardship is indicated by the term "care." "Ground of possibility" is still a metaphysical expression, but it is thought out of the abyssal and steadfast belongingness.[46]

Although, in a certain structural sense, the human is *already* the *Da* of *Sein* (i.e., the place of being's unfolding), it is so *unreflectively* or, worse, while under the enchantment of certain fatal (metaphysical) misunderstandings. The human must move away from these unreflective misunderstandings and *project* itself toward its (proper) role as *Dasein* and move toward that projection as a futural possibility.[47] In his "Running Notes on *Being and Time*," Heidegger puts it the following way:

> In *Being and Time*, *Dasein* and being-human [are] equated – this too is erroneous ... instead, *Dasein* is what ... must originally be gained – what "is" only in this happening of the leap and its building-up. [In *Being and Time*] *Dasein* is taken as the being of humanity and being-human is not itself grasped as the springing open of *Dasein*.[48]

One could put the matter in the following way: the problem with the current human is that it is *too human*, that it is *not enough Dasein*. The contemporary human understands itself as *animale rationale*, a self-(mis)understanding that bespeaks an uncanny alienation from its proper essence. In a very real sense, then, to become *Dasein* is to become *less human* (i.e., it is to earn some distance from the traditional metaphysical conceptions of the human). Thus, while it was stated at the beginning of this section that the human *is Dasein*, it is more accurate to say that the human is that being who has *Dasein* as an essential *possibility*, but who *also* (therefore) *is not yet* that possibility. The human is the one who has not yet appropriated its proper role as the *Da* of *Sein*, the *there* of being's unfolding. The human is, as Heidegger puts it, "the one to come."[49]

Such an appropriation would require a thoroughgoing (re)consideration of being, freeing it from its metaphysical strictures, and this entails thinking the intimate interrelation of world to earth. In this way, coming to be *Dasein* not only *results* in a remembering of the earth – it also *depends* upon such remembering:

---

[45] GA 94: 45–47/34–35. [46] GA 65: 297/234. [47] GA 65: 309/245. [48] GA 82: 22/56.
[49] See Vallega-Neu 2003, 97ff.

> The historical human being of the Western future must be allowed to acquire one thing as what is first: to dwell on this earth poetically, i.e., to build, for the grounding of the truth of beyng, measure and structure in humanity – in order to experience an essential plight, the assignment to being in its question-worthiness.[50]

A movement of the human into its proper essence thus follows upon, or coincides with, the human's reuniting with the earth: "What we await is the occidental essence of the earth and of the human."[51] The proper essence of the human will remain concealed until the earth is experienced and thought in its proper (self-concealing) character.[52]

The question then becomes: *How* will the human come to remember the earth? How will the human get thrust (back) into its role as the *there* of being and (thus) remember earth? Although Heidegger explores various pathways back into such remembering (such as poetry, artworks, and inceptual thinking), there is one path in particular that bears mentioning here. Previously it was stated that the forgetfulness of being has led to the widespread devastation and destitution that characterize the contemporary world. Somewhat ironically, it is, according to Heidegger, precisely this devastation that can best reawaken the human to the means of overcoming it. Drawing on a line from Hölderlin that "where danger is | grows the saving power also," Heidegger argues that it is only as the pernicious effects of technology (and its underlying worldview) reach their most feverish pitch that the human will be thrust back into a cognizant relation to being:

> For the saving power lets the human see and enter into the highest dignity of his essence. This dignity lies in keeping watch over the unconcealment – and with it, from the first, the concealment – of all coming to presence on this earth. It is precisely in enframing, which threatens to sweep the human away into ordering as the supposed single way of revealing, and so thrusts man into the danger of the surrender of his free essence – it is precisely in this extreme danger that the innermost indestructible belongingness of the human within granting may come to light, provided that we, for our part, begin to pay heed to the coming to presence of technology. ... The closer we come to the danger, the more brightly do the ways into the saving power begin to shine and the more questioning we become.[53]

Thus, the very same situation that has led the earth to the brink of actual destruction and already long ago led to a forgetting of the earth (as the concealment operative in being) will *also* lead the human to a salvific commemoration of the earth. Said more concretely, it is the threat of the literal *end of the earth* that is most capable of awaking the human to a commemorative

---

[50] GA 96: 116/91.   [51] GA 97: 50.   [52] See also GA 94: 400/292.   [53] GA 7: 33/337.

awareness of the earth as the concealing ground of being. The human is thus the one who, through the course of exploiting the earth to the point of forgetting the earth entirely, will come to remember the earth precisely from out of such exploitation.[54]

Through such commemoration of the self-concealing earth,[55] the human would come to *shelter* the earth, holding fast to its concealing character so as to resist its passing away into pure oblivion (or, what amounts to the same, into the sheer orderability and manipulability of calculative thinking): in this way, the human would *watch over* the earth, safe-guarding and *protecting* it, becoming a *steward* of the self-concealing earth. Through such stewardship, the human would enter into its destined role as the *there* of being, as *Da-sein* properly understood.

As some of his Black Notebooks make clear, Heidegger comes to think of *Dasein* as consisting precisely of this remembrance of the earth:

> Is Da-sein only a transient streak of lightning beyond the earth, into a world, out of that abyss which contends between world and earth – or do the most secret earth and the most open world first become extant in the "there" of Da-sein?[56]

> Da-sein as the contention of the strife between world and earth.[57]

> The human being is as Da-sein the place of the casting of being (the clearing event of appropriation) into that which then for the first time can step forth as a being – can enter into the strife of world and earth.[58]

> Da-sein, in whose truth for the first time nature and history – in general, a world – come into the open and liberate the earth to its closedness.[59]

Coming to be *Dasein* and coming to know oneself as *Dasein* thus entail coming to know the strife that plays out in (and as) the essence of the human properly understood. To be the human, as *Dasein*, is to serve as the open site of the strife of earth and world (i.e., concealment and unconcealment) that comprises the very heart of being itself, and to shelter such strife.

In light of this, one thinks again of the "Myth of Cura" so central to *Being and Time*, where Care forms the human out of earth. With this myth in mind, one might ask: Does the human's remembrance of the earth, experienced in the face of the earth's destruction, entail becoming mindful of the *earthy* constitution of the human? Would remembering the earth that serves as the concealed ground of the worlding clearing of *Da-sein* also, then, include remembering that the

---

[54] One might think of the growing concern for the earth brought about by the climate crisis as evidence of the veracity of Heidegger's argument.
[55] On this nature of this self-concealing character, see Sallis 2000, 179.   [56] GA 94: 317/230.
[57] GA 94: 333/242.   [58] GA 96: 85/68.   [59] GA 94: 223/163.

human is – as the very name implies – *earthmade*? In the face of the end of the earth, would the human prove itself to be the one who finally comes to know itself, who comes to know its *proper name*, and thereby comes to know the earth?

Such knowing would bring about a new *rootedness* to human *Dasein*, a rootedness in the earth that would overcome the rootlessness of the contemporary forgetfulness of being.[60] The authentic thinking of the unconcealing truth of being "brings [the human] back to the Earth of his homeland – that is, transports him into historical *Dasein* and its Earthly rootedness in a landscape."[61] Those who cultivate this knowledge of the alethic character of being "are those who concomitantly bear *Dasein* as such – and in themselves establish that *Dasein* is to withstand the tumult of truth – alone, trees rooted in the ground, whose mission is to protrude simply into heaven and, in the structure of the clasping and penetrating roots, to preserve the soil from landslides."[62] The human to come is thus the one who will, *like a tree*, root itself firmly in the earth as that which allows it to open up to the expansive air above. Such a future human would thus be

> inclined to the simple things, as is the young birch [*Birke*], which, well disposed to all circumstances and winds, takes into its favor the stars and the sun and greets the earth, whose enclosing power maintains it.[63]

Through becoming aware of the earth at the concealed core of (human) being, through *thinking* this earth, the human would become *like a birch* – or, as he suggests in one of his Black Notebooks, *like a rose*:

> The greatest difficulty of contemplative thinking is to have clear knowledge of its superfluity and nevertheless to carry out such thinking in an essentially still more simple carefreeness than could ever be the one with which the rose radiates its flowering into nature. For the rose has the "bliss" of ignorance – and of something entirely retained in the protection of the closure of the earth.[64]

2 Water: The Sole Catastrophe

The human could never *be* without water. There is, of course, the biological sense in which this is true: the human body is comprised largely of water and needs it, in rather great quantities, to sustain its life. Without the water we pull

---

[60] See GA 16: 521–522/48–49.
[61] GA 52: 182/165. Heidegger is actually speaking directly of *poets* here, i.e., those who endure the direct exposure to the truth of being. However, since the poets do so precisely to ground the future of a new historical Da-sein, I have generalized the point to refer to the human as such.
[62] GA 94: 168/123.   [63] GA 96: 69/54.   [64] GA 96: 130/101.

from taps, wells, and, more often than not these days, from single-use plastic bottles, treating such bottles and the water within them as disposable and infinitely renewable units of standing-reserve, the human organism would wither away and die. In this manner, water is absolutely essential to human life and, indeed, to nearly all life as such.

However, this scientific understanding of water and its importance to (human) life plays very little, if any, role within Heidegger's thought. While he was no doubt aware of the vital importance of water to the human understood as a biological organism, there is a much more fundamental sense in which the human being, in Heidegger's view, needs water. Indeed, it is no exaggeration to say that, for Heidegger, without water the human being could not *be*, in any genuine sense, and that it is only on the basis of water that authentic existence becomes possible for the human. In this way, water is utterly essential to the human, and in a much more elemental sense than the sciences could ever conceive.

The extent to which this is the case is primarily developed by Heidegger during the 1930s and 1940s through his various engagements with the German poet Friedrich Hölderlin. In all of these engagements, though perhaps most pointedly in his 1942 lecture course on "The Ister," Heidegger places great emphasis on the role of water – rivers, in particular – in preparing and making possible the being of the human. For Heidegger, rivers are emblematic of the historical (i.e., temporal) manner by which human beings come to dwell upon the earth, indeed serving as the very possibility of such dwelling.[65] This is certainly the case with actual rivers, which very often serve as the geographical (or hydrographical) site of human dwelling and community. (One sees this quite clearly in Germany, where one finds so many cities, towns, and hamlets – such as Berlin, Tübingen, and Würzburg – built along the banks of rivers, rivers that, in addition to serving as sites of commerce and recreation, imbue each location with its distinctive cultural character and charm.) But Heidegger has something more fundamental than this geographical sense in mind. For Heidegger, rivers make possible what we might call *existential* or *ontological* dwelling, or what he will call *poetic* dwelling. Regarding such dwelling, Heidegger offers the following:

> The river determines the dwelling place of human beings upon the earth. . . . Dwelling takes on an abode and is an abiding in such an abode, specifically that of human beings upon this earth. The abode is a whiling. It needs a while. In such a while, human beings find rest. Yet rest here does not mean the cessation of activity or the halting of disruption. Rest is a grounded repose in

---

[65] See Warminski 1990.

the steadfastness of one's own essence. In rest, the human essence is preserved in its inviolability.[66]

Simply put, rivers allow the human to cultivate the solidity of its own essence, *to dwell* therein, and are, as he puts it in GA 75, *elemental* to such dwelling.[67]

Heidegger proceeds to argue that such dwelling requires a certain *movement* on the part of the human, a multidirectional counterflow of which rivers (or, at least, the Ister) are paradigmatic. Heidegger calls this counter-flowing movement "journeying," where this term denotes the way in which the human, in order to enter into its own proper essence, must first enter into an encounter with what is foreign to it.[68] Heidegger will describe this journeying further as an essential process of *homecoming*, of passing into the foreign for the sake of coming (back) to be at home in one's being.[69] The Ister both literally is and is emblematic of such dwelling and such homecoming, to the extent that it (seemingly) flows backward along its own course and returns to its source. More generally, insofar as a river, as Mitchell puts it, is "at each particular moment connected to both its source and mouth ... so much so, in fact, that the source and the mouth are nothing other than the river itself,"[70] it is demonstrative of authentic human temporality, which orients itself in a unified and sustained way both to what has come (i.e., the past) and what, on the bases of such, is yet to come (i.e., the future).[71] Rivers are expressive of this authentic temporality – or, rather, they just *are* such temporality: "The rivers intimate and vanish into time and do so in such a way that they themselves are thus of time and are time itself."[72]

Heidegger's meditation on this movement of homecoming plays out in two interrelated registers, namely the *political* and the *ontological*. Regarding the political sense, Heidegger argues that Germans in particular must travel into the foreign of ancient Greece (by way of an intellectual, poetic excursion) in order to appropriate their own historical essence: Germany's sense of identity, its appropriation of its historical destiny, depends upon it.[73] Regarding the deeper, ontological sense, Heidegger argues that the human *as such* must (re)enter into a primordial exposure to *being* – that is, the source of its essence. Drawing upon the first choral ode from Sophocles' *Antigone*, with which (according to Heidegger) Hölderlin's river poetry bears an essential and complementary affinity, Heidegger shows how the human is most at home in the particular beings with which it finds itself; however, precisely by feeling at home among such beings, the human is cut off from what is most essential for it, namely

---

[66] GA 53: 23/20. [67] See GA 75: 64. [68] See GA 53: 61/49. See Richardson 2003, 450.
[69] See Winkler 2017, 383. [70] Mitchell 2015, 93.
[71] See Hoy in Miller 2008, 264–265; see also Gosetti-Ferencei 2004, 94. [72] GA 53: 12/12.
[73] GA 53: 67/54. See Savage 2008, 50.

being itself. In this way, the latter is the foreign into which the human must travel in order to find (and found) its proper essence, its ownmost *Dasein*. Like a river, the human must journey back toward its alienated source, its estranged element.

All of this implies, of course, that the human is, at least initially and for the most part, *not* at home in (its) being. Such seems to follow necessarily, even *lawfully* or *logically*, from Heidegger's understanding of the structure of "what is one's own":

> One's own is least of all something that produces itself of its own accord. One's own must come to be appropriate. And in turn, whatever has become appropriate needs to be appropriated. All this is true only on the presupposition that initially human beings are not and indeed never "of themselves," or through any self-making, in that which is their own. In that case, however, to dwell in what is one's own is what comes last and is seldom successful and always remains what is most difficult.[74]

The human is thus not (yet) settled within its essence, but of necessity must journey a difficult path toward that essence.[75] In this way, as Heidegger argues, the human is essentially characterized by a certain *not being-at-home*: "this coming to be at home in one's own in itself entails that human beings are initially, and for a long time, and sometimes forever, not at home."[76] In other words, the human – to begin with, *and perhaps even forever* – is *essentially homeless*.[77] (One might relate this to what was said in the previous section about the manner in which the human is *not yet Dasein*, having not yet entered into its proper essence: this "not yet" seems to belong to the essential character of the human.)

Still drawing on the language of Sophocles' choral ode, Heidegger casts this homelessness in terms of "uncanniness" (*Unheimlichkeit*), where one is meant to hear in this word a semantic and philosophical connection to "home" (*Heim*).[78] For Heidegger, the human is the most uncanny of beings insofar as it is essentially cast out of that to which it most belongs, finding itself at home precisely in that which most alienates it from its proper home, seeking refuge and dwelling in *beings* in such a manner as to (thereby) forget *being*.[79] In so turning toward beings, the human turns *away* from what is most essential to itself, thereby further alienating itself from its proper essence. Heidegger describes this uncanny situation in the following remarkable way:

---

[74] GA 53: 21/24.
[75] See GA 52:188/160, where Heidegger expressly ties the journey of homecoming to the sea: "To finding one's own there belongs the sea voyage."
[76] GA 53: 60/49.   [77] See Gosetti-Ferencei 2004, 176.   [78] See GA 53: 87/81.
[79] See Capobianco 2010, 63.

> The uncanniness of the unhomely here consists in the fact that human beings themselves in their essence are a καταστροφή – a reversal that turns them away from their own essence. Among beings, the human being is the sole catastrophe.[80]

The human is "the sole catastrophe": it is, in its very core, a *reversal*, a *turning around*, an *inversion*. The human is, in its very essence, a turning around or inverting of that essence, not at all unlike the Ister which seemingly flows backward upon itself and into its source. Such a reversal is carried out, for example, in the manner in which the human – the only entity for Heidegger who can *know* being in any meaningful sense – continually forgets being. (This is, of course, ultimately owing to the alethic character of being itself, i.e., the manner in which it entails an essential element of withdrawing concealment.) The human is, in this way, the uncanny site of the forgetfulness *and* the (possible) remembrance of being: the human is the site of the monstrous marriage of forgetting and remembering, revealing and concealing, essence and unessence.[81]

Heidegger speaks further of this catastrophic character of the human being in his 1943 lectures on Heraclitus. Interestingly, he there casts this catastrophe in terms of *water*:

> Let us imagine, if only for a few minutes, what would become of the human if it came about that every possibility of saying and understanding the words "is" and "being" were revoked. No catastrophe that could befall the planet can be compared with this seemingly most trivial of events in which the human's relation to "is" is suddenly suspended. But this catastrophe has long since arrived, only no one has noticed it in its essence. The human, in its history, has reached the point where he has forgotten the "is" and "being," insofar as he renounces any consideration of what is named by this word. Indifference to "being" has besieged the planet. The human being allows himself to be washed over by the flood of this forgetfulness of being [*Der Mensch läßt sich von der Flut der Seinsvergessenheit überspülen*]. But, in truth, this is not even a "diving into" the flood [*ein Untertauchen in dieser Flut*] anymore, for that would still require an awareness of the forgetfulness of being. Precisely this forgetfulness of being has itself already been forgotten, which is surely in accordance with the essence of forgetting, sucking up everything in its radius like an undertow [*Sog*].[82]

The human, the sole entity capable of knowing being, has been washed over by the forgetfulness of being, has *let* itself be drowned in this way, and so much so as to have forgotten the forgetting. In this way, the human is the site of the

---

[80] GA 53: 77/94. [81] On the catastrophe of the human, see Withy in Wrathall 2021, 790.
[82] GA 55: 83/62.

greatest catastrophe that can befall the planet, or is itself that greatest catastrophe: the human *is* the carrying out of the catastrophic forgetting of being, and thus of its own essence.

Rivers, according to Heidegger, mitigate this catastrophe to some extent, helping prepare the site wherein the human can enter into its proper essence (i.e., by remembering being) and find repose:

> Yet if the river determines the locality of the homely, then it is of essential assistance in becoming homely in what is one's own. By "assistance" we understand here not some occasional support but something steadfastly standing by, this word taken in the full force of its naming, meaning that the river is in advance and everywhere there-by [*da-bei*] and "there" ["*da*"].[83]

Thus, rivers aid in bringing the human to itself, into founding its proper dwelling, by serving as the place, the *there* (*Da*), of such dwelling.[84] In this way, rivers are a literal embodiment of the sort of commemorative thinking required for the human to (re)enter into its essence. Rivers can, in this sense, *save* the human from (its own) catastrophe, turning it back toward that from which it, by its very essence, turns away. Somewhat ironically, then, rivers can save the human from being drowned in the flood of the forgetfulness of being.

As Heidegger argues within the lecture course, this foundational, commemorative, salvific role of rivers is to be understood as comparable – or, indeed, as *identical* – to that of *poets*:

> Yet the rivers are the poets who found the poetic, upon whose ground human beings dwell. The poetic spirit of the river makes arable in an essential sense: it prepares the ground for the hearth of the house of history. The poet opens that time-space within which a belonging to the hearth and a being homely is possible in general.[85]

Just as a river "makes arable" a geographical location, thereby inaugurating an event of physical and cultural founding, so too do poets prepare an existential and historical site for human community. As Vallega-Neu explains it, "the creative ones are ... poets, thinkers, and founders of states who, disposed by a basic

---

[83] GA 53: 24/21.

[84] GA 53: 31/27: "The river gives us a possible 'here' – a locale: in giving the locale, the river prevails over the essence of the locale, that is, its locality. Who those are who say 'Here, however, we wish to build,' at first remains obscure. Presumably they are human beings, or beings akin to humans."

[85] GA 53: 187/147. See also GA 39: 264/239: "The river is not a body of water that simply flows past the locale of human beings; rather, its flowing, as land-forming, first creates the possibility of grounding the dwellings of humans. The river is a founder and poet [*Stifter und Dichter*], not just metaphorically, but as itself."

attunement ... create the spaces for future historical beyng of a people."[86] (They do this by defining a cultural, spiritual horizon in terms of which a community or even epoch can understand itself.) Heidegger himself offers the most succinct (if somewhat baffling) formulation when he writes that "the poet is the river and the river is the poet."[87] Both rivers and poets, if one can even speak of them as different entities (in light of the above identification), open up a world in which authentic human dwelling becomes possible, a world in which the human can overcome (by some measure) its forgetfulness of being and (re)enter into its proper essence.

Of course, whereas actual rivers carry out their founding by means of the *water* of which they are comprised, poets carry out their founding (i.e., their commemoration) by means of *words* – that is, they do so by means of *poetry*. (One thinks of Hölderlin for Heidegger and the Germans, but no less of Homer or Sophocles for the Greeks.) And yet there is every indication that Heidegger thinks of poetry in terms of *water* – or, indeed, simply *as* water.[88] Heidegger indicates as much during an analysis of Hölderlin's poetry in *What Is Called Thinking*:

> Memory, Mother of the Muses – the thinking back to what is to be thought is the source and ground of poesy. This is why poesy is the water [*das Gewässer*] that at times flows backward to the source, toward thinking as a thinking back, recollection.[89]

Poetry, as commemorative thinking, is like a river moving back to its source: or, rather, such poetry is not *like* the river – it *is* the river.[90] Poetry draws the human (back) commemoratively toward its proper essence, enabling the human to found and cultivate its authentic dwelling.

With this, Heidegger indicates a certain kinship between *language* and *water*. Yet how would one begin to make sense of this strange kinship? One could perhaps gain clarity on this issue by turning to "The Letter on Humanism," penned by Heidegger in 1946. From the very outset, this essay is focused on language and the manner in which the human, and *only* the human, dwells within it. Throughout Heidegger's corpus, the human is again and again said to be the only being "with" language; as Heidegger famously puts it, "language is

---

[86] Vallega-Neu 2018, 10. See also Bambach 2022, 78: "In much the same way as poetry founds being in words, rivers found being as dwelling."
[87] GA 53: 203/165. [88] See GA 75: 259. [89] GA 8: 13/11.
[90] One way to understand Heidegger's claim regarding the identity of poets and rivers is as follows. Because the being of rivers only first comes to language *through* the poet – that is, through an exemplary experience of *language* – it is principally *as poetry* that the rivers carry out their preparation of human dwelling. In other words, rivers *primarily* found human dwelling by way of language, since it is the poets who *first* articulate the essence of rivers. Because we do not even know what a river *is* without poets, the foundational operations of the latter depend upon that of the former. On this, see Winkler 2017, 371. See also Murray 1980, 54.

the house of Being; in its home the human dwells."[91] As the human's place of dwelling, language is "the home of the human's essence" in that it is only through language that the human carries out and comes into contact with its role as the place of being's clearing.[92] As "the clearing-concealing advent of Being itself," language is how a world of experience and meaningfulness opens for the human: it is the originary dimension in or through which the human comes into contact with being and beings, and is indeed the very open(ing) of being itself.[93]

However, for the most part, and owing especially to the pernicious influence of metaphysical thinking (which is nothing other than the concrete enactment of the forgetfulness of being), the human has misunderstood the nature of language, taking it to consist in mere verbal expression, communication, and (idle) talk. Regarding this state of affairs, Heidegger writes that

> the downfall of language is... not the grounds for, but already a consequence of, the state of affairs in which language under the dominance of the modern metaphysics of subjectivity almost irremediably *falls out of its element* [*aus ihrem Element herausfällt*]. Language still denies us its essence: that it is the house of the truth of Being.[94]

In taking language in the superficial (and derivative) sense as a *technique* of verbal or written communication,[95] the human thereby loses touch with language as the emerging clearing of being, and language itself "falls out of its element" – that is, it loses contact with being. Only by *thinking* can the human enter back into a proper comportment toward language and (thereby) into the element of being.

However, as Heidegger makes abundantly clear, the human being, despite being the sole entity capable of thinking, is *not yet* thinking –[96] that is, the human has yet to enter into its proper element. Regarding this uncanny situation, Heidegger offers the following:

> Being, as the element of thinking [*das Element des Denkens*], is abandoned by the technical interpretation of thinking. "Logic," beginning with the Sophists and Plato, sanctions this explanation. Thinking is judged by a standard that does not measure up to it. Such judgment may be compared to the procedure of trying to evaluate the essence and powers of a fish [*des Fisches*] by seeing how long it can live on dry land. For a long time now, all too long, thinking has been stranded on dry land [*dem Trockenen*].[97]

---

[91] GA 9: 313/217. [92] GA 9: 333/237.
[93] See GA 79: 71/67: "Language is the inceptual dimension [*anfängliche Dimension*] within which the human essence is first capable of corresponding to being and its claim and of belonging to being through this correspondence. This inceptual correspondence, properly enacted, is thinking. By thinking we first learn to dwell in the realm in which the conversion of the dispensation of being, the conversion of positionality, takes place."
[94] GA 9: 318/222–223. [95] See GA 52: 10/8. [96] GA 8: 5/8. [97] GA 9: 315/219.

Thinking, *like a fish out of water*, has slipped out of its element.[98] Of course, as Heidegger will argue, *being* is the proper element of thinking, the element out of which thinking, owing to metaphysics, has slipped. Such an image implies that the very element of thinking – namely being itself – is to be thought in terms of water. Only by returning to this element, to being, would thinking be able to return to, and thereby *be*, its proper self: for being is what will "preserve [the human] in its essence, ... maintain it in its element."[99] Only by returning to this element will the human be able to dwell authentically in its proper essence.

But, one can ask: *Why* is language, as the unfolding of being, to be thought in terms of water? What, for Heidegger, is the connection? Heidegger nowhere offers a direct answer to this. However, based on various texts, one can perhaps piece together an explanation. As Heidegger writes in *What Is Called Thinking* (1951–1952), language is characterized by a certain dual nature, on the one hand lending itself to standardized and univocal expressions (i.e., familiar, everyday speech) and on the other hand preserving within itself an inexhaustibility of possible meanings (i.e., poetic expression). For Heidegger, "a wide range of meaning belongs generally to the nature of every word. This ... arises from the mystery of language."[100] Because of this wide range of meaning, to move within language "means moving on shifting ground or, still better, on *the billowing waters of an ocean* [*Wellengang eines Meeres*]."[101] Like the ocean, whose surface shifts about from unstable form to unstable form, language is characterized by a protean dynamism that resists the attempts to pin its meanings down into single, reproducible, and stable forms. Because of this *fluidity*, language remains essentially ambiguous, and this "multiplicity of meanings is the element [*das Element*] in which all thought must move in order to be strict thought."[102]

To help elucidate this point, Heidegger again offers the image of a fish in water:

To use an image: to a fish, the depths and expanses of its waters, the currents and quiet

> pools, warm and cold layers are the element of its multiple mobility [*das Element seiner vielfältigen Beweglichkeit*]. If the fish is deprived of the fullness of its element [*der Fülle seines Elementes*], if it is dragged on the dry sand, then it can only wriggle, twitch, and die. Therefore, we always must seek out thinking, and its burden of thought, in the element of its multiple meanings [*im Element seiner Mehrdeutigkeit*], else everything will remain closed to us.[103]

---

[98] See Richardson 2003, 542. [99] GA 9: 317/220. [100] GA 8: 195/191.
[101] GA 8: 196/192; my italics. [102] GA 8: 75/71. [103] GA 8: 75/71.

To enter back into its proper element, then, thinking must seek after and embrace the essential ambiguities of language, precisely as logic, and metaphysical thinking more broadly, have failed to do. Thinking is most at home, most in its element, in the rich, *fluidic* polyvalence of language.

In his lecture course on Hölderlin's "Remembrance" (1941–1942), Heidegger will speak of such polyvalence in terms of "wealth [*Reichtum*]":

> The wealth belonging to every genuine word – which is emphatically never a mere jumble of scattered meanings but rather the simple unity of what is essential – has its ground in the fact that it names something inceptual, and every commencement is at once inexhaustible and singular.[104]

Such wealth is above all characterized by a *limitless* significance, an *inexhaustible* ambiguity, that extends beyond mere polysemy and requires a special kind of (poetic) thinking that binds itself to a different law than that which governs logical thinking.[105] Perhaps not surprisingly, Heidegger understands such wealth, such superfluity of meaning, in terms of water: "For wealth indeed begins in the ocean."[106] For Heidegger, drawing on Hölderlin, the ocean is emblematic of the superabundant and inexhaustible resources offered by language, the manner in which it lends itself to infinite interpretations. It is across this ocean of meaning that the poet, and those who wish to dwell poetically, must travel in order to enter into their own proper essence.[107]

Thinking must slip back into its proper element of language, properly understood, in order for the human to enter (back into) a mindful dwelling within its proper essence: and it is the poet who, above all, will guide the human toward such dwelling.[108] In "The Letter on Humanism," Heidegger clarifies the character of such dwelling by tying it explicitly to his discussion of dwelling in *Being and Time* almost two decades years earlier:

> This dwelling is the essence of "being-in-the-world." The reference in *Being and Time* (p. 54) to "being-in" as "dwelling" is no etymological game.[109]

In the passage from *Being and Time* referenced here, Heidegger distinguishes the kind of *being-in* that characterizes *Dasein* from the sort of spatial locatedness in terms of which one at-hand entity can be said to be *in* another, such as when one says – and this is Heidegger's example – that "water is 'in' the

---

[104] GA 52: 15/12. [105] GA 52: 26/22. [106] GA 52: 149/175. See also GA 4: 66/88.
[107] See GA 52: 175/149.
[108] Interestingly, *thinking* itself, as Heidegger suggests in the passage from the following poem (from 1946), is to be thought in terms of water: "Thinking is the shy defense | is the cool drink | on the path the soft afterblaze | of lights without number | alike roses | that never fade, | hailing vales and rivers" (GA 81: 22/35).
[109] GA 9: 358/260.

glass."[110] The manner of being-in that characterizes *Dasein* is instead to be understood in terms of residing (*Aufhalten*) amongst things, being among them, being familiar with them, being, one might say, *at home* with them, diffused amongst them, even *comprised* of them.[111]

In order to attain to its proper *being-in*, its authentic *being-at-home*, the human needs the exposure to the waters of language brought about by the poet. Heidegger indicates as much in a passage from GA 75, where he again indicates that he understands Hölderlin's notion of "dwelling" (*Wohnen*) in terms of the essential existential state of "being-in" as it is developed in *Being and Time*. Under the heading "Hölderlin's word 'dwelling,'" Heidegger offers the following: "See *Being and Time*, page 54: *innan* – being-in; as dwelling; *habitare* – *diligere*."[112] And then he adds, most remarkably, "*Dwelling and water* [*Wohnen und Wasser*]," thus indicating an essential connection between the two. The human *needs* water, understood poetically, in order to dwell on this earth. The human needs to be exposed to the fluidic ocean of language in order to find (and found) its proper abode.

As an aside, and in light of Heidegger's comment here, one wonders: Could one find such a connection between water and *Dasein* in *Being and Time*? That is, if one reread *Being and Time* after having read Heidegger's engagement with Hölderlin's river poetry, would one be able to discern some sense in which *Dasein*, even within the pages of *Being and Time*, bore an essential connection to water? To hazard an answer to this, one might return to the "Myth of Cura" that serves as the litmus test of Heidegger's proposal that *care* serves as the ground of the being of *Dasein*. As we saw in the previous section, this story – a story that is, in the most profound sense, a *poem* – refers to the elemental (albeit concealed) role that earth plays in the constitution of *Dasein*. But it also refers to *water*. Indeed, the very first line of this poem mentions water, and a river in particular: "Once, when Cura was crossing a river, she saw some clay."[113] It is this river clay that Cura picks up and forms into the shape that will become characteristic of the human. The word Stambaugh translates as "clay" is *Erdreich*, which means, more literally, a *rich* earth or soil. But, given that Cura is crossing a river, Stambaugh is right to translate it as "clay": one imagines the wet, pliable earth that one finds along a river, a soil malleable enough to be formed into a shape that, by virtue of its dampness, it is able to hold. According to this story, water is elemental to *Dasein* to exactly the same extent, and in exactly the same way, that earth is. Alongside earth, water is an essential element out of which *Dasein*, the being who *cares*, is comprised. Said otherwise: water is *implicit* in the earth out of which the human is formed.

---

[110] GA 2: 72/79.   [111] See Richardson 2003, 52.   [112] GA 75: 385.   [113] GA 2: 262/242.

But what, if anything, would this mean for Heidegger's analytic of *Dasein* within *Being and Time*? Given Heidegger's pairing of water and language analyzed above, one might want to infer from this that language, within the perimeters of *Being and Time*, serves as an essential element of *Dasein*'s being in the same manner that it does in "The Letter on Humanism" and in Heidegger's meditations on Hölderlin. However, Heidegger does not employ the metaphorics of water in *Being and Time*;[114] moreover, language does not occupy the pride of place within *Being and Time* that it will come to occupy in his later thinking. Nevertheless, language does play a crucial role within the text, and is, as Hatab puts it, "equiprimordial with all other elements of *Dasein*'s disclosedness" and is "co-determinative with understanding and mood."[115] Simply put, language is one of the ways by which *Dasein* cares for the things amongst which it finds itself and by means of which it navigates its world.

And yet there is an annotation, added by Heidegger sometime later, that suggests that language is meant to be more than just one other element among others. During his discussion of *significance* as the interlocking totality of relationships that structure *Dasein*'s being-in-the-world, Heidegger offers the following regarding the relationship between words (i.e., language) and signification:

> the significance itself with which Da-sein is always already familiar contains the ontological condition of the possibility that Da-sein, understanding, and interpreting can disclose something akin to "significations" which in turn found the possible being of words and language.[116]

The suggestion here is that words/language are subsequent to and rendered possible by the underlying scaffolding of signification serving as the basic structure of being in the world. And yet Heidegger later added the following footnote to the final word in the sentence (i.e., "language"): "Untrue. Language is not imposed but *is* the primordial essence of truth as there (*Da*)."[117] This indicates that Heidegger later came to see the role of language as much more primordial and, indeed, as replacing "signification" as the foundational structure of being-in-the-world. Language is thus not one mode of disclosure among others: it is the primordial essence – the very element, we might say – of the *there*, of the open, of the clearing. Language is *how* the human, as the *there* of being, unfolds: the human is utterly *immersed* in it.

---

[114] There is one exception to this. While discussing the fallenness of *Dasein*, Heidegger describes the movement of falling prey (to the They) as *Wirbel*: "eddying," "swirling," or "washing away" (GA 2: 237/167). The human is sucked into the They as though through a swirling whirlpool.
[115] Hatab in Wrathall 2021, 448.   [116] GA 2: 117/82.   [117] GA 2: 117/82.

Thus, despite not *being-in* in the sense of water in a glass, *Dasein*'s peculiar *being-in* must nonetheless be thought of as bearing some essential connection to water. As we have seen, this connection must be understood as suggestive of the way in which the human must cultivate a more authentic relation to language. As we have also seen, it is the poets – whom Heidegger elsewhere describes as "seafarers"[118] – who are needed to draw the human back toward the source, to bring the human back into a proper comportment toward language. By "liberating" language from grammar and logic (i.e., metaphysics), poets are able to reawaken the human's awareness of being, thereby bringing the human back into its proper element, an element it has slipped out of "like a fish out of water."[119] Such liberation is needed in order to prepare the site of human existence for a proper dwelling, a proper *being-in*, within the truth of being.

As a concrete example of what such liberation would look like, one can turn to "The Question Concerning Technology," where Heidegger argues that modern technology, in presenting beings as standing-reserve (i.e., as on call for human ordering and use), has cut the human off from a more primordial experience of the being of beings. Using the example of the Rhine river to make his case, Heidegger offers the following:

> The hydroelectric plant is set [*gestellt*] into the current of the Rhine. It sets [*stellt*] the Rhine to supplying its hydraulic pressure, which then sets [*stellt*] the turbines turning. This turning sets those machines in motion whose thrust sets [*herstellt*] going the electric current for which the long-distance power station and its network of cables are set up [*bestellt*] to dispatch electricity. In the context of the interlocking processes pertaining to the orderly disposition of electrical energy, even the Rhine itself appears as something at our command. The hydroelectric plant is not built into the Rhine River as was the old wooden bridge that joined bank with bank for hundreds of years. Rather the river is dammed up into the power plant. What the river is now, namely, a water power supplier, derives from out of the essence of the power station. In order that we may even remotely consider the monstrousness that reigns here, let us ponder for a moment the contrast that speaks out of the two titles, "The Rhine" as dammed up into the power works, and "The Rhine" as uttered out of the artwork, in Hölderlin's hymn by that name.[120]

As this passage indicates, the age of enframing has brought about a situation where the human, having forgotten the inceptual meaning of being, relates to beings – including natural beings such as rivers – only as standing-reserve (i.e., only instrumentally). It is this situation which, according to Heidegger, has

---

[118] GA 53: 180/153.
[119] GA 9: 314/218: "The liberation of language from grammar into a more original essential framework is reserved for thought and poetic creation." See Richardson 2003, 22.
[120] GA 7: 16/321.

brought the human to the very brink of global catastrophe. As this passage further suggests, it is poetry – and, specifically, poetry about water – that is needed to reawaken the human to the meaning of being, and thereby to save the human from destruction.

However, it is not only the poets who can draw the human back into an appropriate relation to being: *it is water itself*. As Heidegger argues in the Bremen lectures, *things*, in the special sense to which he gives the term, are capable of drawing the human out of its immersion in representational metaphysics and reawakening it to the primordial clearing of being. Using a jug as his example, Heidegger shows how a *thing*, once grasped in a manner no longer bound by representational metaphysics, is capable of drawing the human's attention to the fourfold – that is, the manner of being's opening into the quadrants of earth, mortal, sky, and divinity. The jug – which Heidegger specifies is for "wine or water" – carries out, in this manner, an operation of poetic manifestation, allowing the very process of phenomenality to show itself. At the very end of his analysis, Heidegger enumerates several other *things* capable of drawing attention to the fourfold unfolding of being, including "pond and stream."[121] Bodies of water, then, are *also* able to draw the human's attention to the fourfold and thus (re)awaken the human to the otherwise forgotten clearing of being. Or, at least, they are able to do this *if* the human relates to them not as standing-reserve but as the foundations upon or around which it can cultivate its existential dwelling, a relation that is (re)awakened for the human through the work of the poets. In other words, the Rhine river *itself*, when poetically conceived, is capable of alerting the human to the heretofore forgotten character of being itself.

The human of the contemporary world is thus that one who, accustomed to the technological representation of both water and language as standing-reserve, must learn to relate to both in a more inceptual way, namely as the very foundation of human dwelling. The human is thus the one who, not *yet* at home, must leap headlong into the billowing ocean of language and thereby into its proper element.[122] Once in touch with language, its essential source, the human would be like that birch tree (*Birke*) mentioned at the end of the previous section, a tree whose roots would be fed by the waters of being:

> "Birch down by the water
> hush your leafy whisper
> twisting through the dreaming hours
> of my ungodly soul,

---

[121] GA 79: 21/20.   [122] See GA 79: 163/154.

which, aquiver,
a lily-of-the-pond,
can hardly bear the plunge and wring
of its lurching waves!"

— Heidegger, 1910[123]

3 Air: The Sign

The human is *surrounded* by air. This, at least, is what modern science tells us. For the scientist, the earth is surrounded by an admixture of oxygen and nitrogen, the invisible presence of which is necessary for the existence of the human (and not only the human). During its earthy sojourn, the human needs to remain in contact with this air, enveloped in it, *drawing it in and out* in order to remain alive. Indeed, even when the human *leaves* the earth – as it is perhaps one day destined to do entirely – it must take such air with itself, enveloping itself, or at least its nose and mouth, in an artificial atmosphere of air.

As one might expect, Heidegger views this scientific understanding of air as problematic – indeed, he views it as a symptom of the most extreme *danger* that confronts the human. This is owing to the fact that such an understanding of air (as a mixture of chemicals), based as it is on the representational metaphysics characteristic of the West, reduces air to a unit of standing-reserve, to little more than a storehouse for the useful chemicals out of which it is comprised: "Air is now set upon to yield nitrogen."[124] It is this view of nature as infinitely exploitable and manipulatable that has brought the human to the brink of planetary collapse – and, what's worse (according to Heidegger), to the point where being itself has been almost entirely forgotten.[125] The forgetting of air as anything more than an invisible but omnipresent storehouse of fuel – or, for example, as a medium of mass transportation[126] – is symptomatic of the forgetfulness of being that characterizes the contemporary era and that threatens to destroy the very humanity of the human.

Although it has been alleged that Heidegger himself forgot about air,[127] air plays an important, albeit largely invisible, role within Heidegger's 1943–1944 lectures on Heraclitus. At the risk of reducing two extraordinarily complex lecture courses into coarsely conceived themes, it can be said that the 1943 lecture course focuses on the role of φύσις within Heraclitus's thought, while the 1944 course focuses on the role of λόγος, and, although it has been

---
[123] GA 81: 5/5.   [124] GA 7: 16/320.   [125] See, for example, GA 55: 106/79.
[126] See GA 55: 106/79.
[127] Irigaray argues that Heidegger overlooked the role of air in the elemental experience of the human (Irigaray 1999). As rich and as otherwise compelling as her book is, it contains two major lacunae: she deals with neither Heidegger's work on Hölderlin nor on Heraclitus, both of which, as will come to light in what follows, contain rich meditations on the role of air in human life.

almost entirely overlooked, air plays an elemental role in both of these courses. Indeed, air proves to be an essential element of both *being* (understood as φύσις) and the human (as the entity with λόγος) inceptually understood. As we will see in what follows, the human, as that being who stands within the clearing of being in such a way as to gather itself to that clearing, remains permeated and surrounded, if not indeed partially constituted, by air.

The first mention of air occurs near the beginning of the 1943 lecture course. Heidegger relays two stories regarding the inceptual thinker Heraclitus. The first story appears in Aristotle's *Parts of Animals*; Heidegger, with some minor insertions of his own, recounts it as follows:

> Regarding Heraclitus the following (story) is recounted: namely, that he spoke to the visitors who wanted to approach him. Coming closer they saw him as he warmed himself at an oven. They remained standing there (very surprised by this), on account of the fact that he bid them (including those who were still hesitating) to have courage and come in, calling with the words: "Here, too, the gods are present."[128]

The second story, told by Diogenes Laertius, consists of the following:

> But he had himself withdrawn into the temple of Artemis in order to play knucklebones with the children; here, the Ephesians stood around him, and he said to them: "What are you gaping at, you scoundrels? Or is it not better to do this than to work with you on behalf of the πόλις?"[129]

Neither story has to do with air, at least not directly: indeed, on Heidegger's reading, the first story concerns itself with *fire* (of which we will speak in the following section), the second with *play*. And yet Heidegger will go on to interpret these stories in such a way as to suggest that there is something more fundamental to them that has, through their traditional interpretations, been overlooked. As we will soon see, this has *everything* to do with air.

After having presented and analyzed these two stories, Heidegger reemphasizes that the point of the lecture course is "to become attentive to the word of Heraclitus's."[130] Doing this, Heidegger says, requires that we "experience straightaway the atmosphere [*Atmosphäre*] in which the word of Heraclitus's was said."[131] Regarding such atmosphere – a word that already, in its very etymology, refers to air, to *breathing* – Heidegger offers the following:

> Because Heraclitus is a thinker, the air [*Luft*] that envelopes him is the crisp and cool air [*Luft*] of thoughtful thinking, which is itself a daring deed. The two "stories" concerning Heraclitus should help bring it about that perhaps,

---

[128] GA 55: 6/8. [129] GA 55: 10/10. [130] GA 55: 21/22. [131] GA 55: 22/18.

from time to time, we feel the draft of this air [*Luftzug dieser Luft*], if only from out of the farthest distance.[132]

Owing to the fact that Heraclitus is a *thinker*, in the robust sense that Heidegger develops within the course, the air that envelops him, that wafts and blows around him, is "the crisp cool air" of a certain kind of thinking, namely *thoughtful* thinking (*denkerische Denken*), a thinking that precedes and makes possible the conventional, metaphysical thinking to which we are accustomed, a thinking thus not bound to such metaphysical thinking and its toxic atmosphere, an *inceptual* thinking that attempts to "think in the region of the inception."[133] Coming into greater proximity to Heraclitus's word – coming, that is, into greater nearness to his inceptual thinking – would entail feeling the draft of the air or atmosphere of such thinking, would indeed consist of being drawn into the draft of that thinking, pulled away from the calculative thinking characteristic of the contemporary age and into the region of the inception. Indeed, being drawn into such a draft is the very purpose of the lecture courses, and to this extent they are oriented, overall and from the very outset, toward air.

But what *is* this atmosphere? What, exactly, *is* this air? And where does one find it? Or, as Heidegger himself asks, "Where, in either of these stories, is there a trace of the crisp and cool air from which hails the daring deed that is called 'thinking'"?[134]

Heidegger gives next to nothing by way of a positive response to this question. One could, of course, *infer* the presence of air in both stories about Heraclitus: for, after all, fire needs air to burn,[135] and the *place* of a god – that is, a temple – is nothing other than an open space of air in which a statue of a goddess may show forth and take (or make) place.[136] But Heidegger has neither the air of combustion nor of physical spacing in mind, at least not explicitly. Instead, he only offers a few oblique comments to help us get closer to this elusive air of Heraclitus's thoughtful thinking. He begins by marking the difficulty in finding such air:

> Regarding the manner and the essence of the thinker, and regarding his thinking, nothing shows itself, at least not immediately, and certainly not for the mere gaping eye of the crowd: for this eye sees only what falls immediately in front of it, and only what is obvious and pleasing to it. This eye of the crowd is not inclined to notice what the appearance points to beyond itself. This eye of the crowd is not at all practiced at following what such a pointing points to in each case. The eye of the crowd is blind to signs.[137]

---

[132] GA 55: 22/18. [133] GA 55: 4/4. [134] GA 55: 22/19. [135] See Irigaray 1999, 15.
[136] GA 5: 27/167. [137] GA 55: 23/19.

What is thoughtful about Heraclitus's thinking remains hard to see, almost as though it, *like air*, is invisible except only to those who know what to look for, who know how to read it (*like a sign*). (Most humans – and, indeed, maybe *all* humans, *initially and for the most part* – do not know how to look for it; hence the need for poets and inceptual thinkers.) However, those practiced in such seeing have developed an eye for the *inconspicuous* (*Unauffällige*) that stands behind – or, perhaps, *in front of* – the conspicuous. Such people observe how what is familiar within Heraclitus's thinking points to something unfamiliar, how the oven points to "fire and, in the 'fire,' to glowing and brightness,"[138] and how the game in which Heraclitus is engaged in the second story "points to the relaxed and easy-going, to the dynamism and freedom of play which, as play, nonetheless has its rule and its law."[139] Behind the fire, as it were – or, perhaps, at its very core – a glowing brightness radiates; behind the game, unfettered play reigns. In a manner yet to be clarified, the inconspicuous glow of fire and lawfully free play both point to, or hail from, the "crisp cool air" of thinking. It is as though one, by getting closer to the core of fire and play (and their interconnection), would also gain closer proximity to air.

As Heidegger will go on to argue within the lecture course, fire, understood in terms of the Greek πῦρ, is one of Heraclitus's thoughtful words for *being* (alongside φύσις and ζωή, to name only two others).[140] Likewise, *play* ultimately refers to the dynamic intercourse between emerging and self-concealing that characterizes the essence of φύσις, the essence of life, and (thus) the essence of being itself. Ultimately, both fire and play refer to *being* understood in terms of the inceptual experience of ἀλήθεια, and it is *this* – namely being itself – that is the inconspicuous atmosphere of Heraclitus's thinking, an atmosphere of which one can become aware, provided one knows how to look. Being itself, then, is the "crisp cool air of thinking," and it is within the draft of such air that Heraclitus's inceptual thinking operates.

But how is *being* understood here? And would *air* in any way continue to operate within such an understanding? Would "the crisp cool air" belonging to being prove to be anything more than a metaphor?

On the meaning of being for inceptual thinking, Heidegger is uncharacteristically unambiguous: being is to be understood as the clearing (*die Lichtung*).[141] The clearing is the "illuminating and opening sheltering" through which (or as which) beings come to presence:[142] it is the open emergence in which the human, and *only* the human, is capable of standing steadfastly. Although Heidegger will often describe this clearing in terms of *light*, of *brightening*

---

[138] On the difference between light and glow, see GA 15: 20/8.   [139] GA 55: 23/19.
[140] GA 55: 161/122.   [141] GA 55: 17/15.   [142] GA 55: 17/15.

and *glowing* (which one can hear in the word "illuminating"), it is also, through its connection to the *open*, held in an ineradicable connection with the air. This is perhaps most evident as Heidegger brings the clearing into connection with the inceptual understanding of μέτρον ("measure"): "The fundamental meaning of μέτρον ... is the expanse, the open, the sprawling and widening clearing." Such a sprawling expanse – namely the open expanse of being – is unthinkable without air. Air is the very element in and as which such expansive clearing unfolds and which the illuming proper to the clearing makes visible, serving as the medium of both light and sound. As beings emerge in(to) being, they expand into (and as) the clearing, the capacious and airy open of being.

One can perhaps see this in more concrete detail by turning to Heidegger's mention of the water of a spring "emerging into the light of day."[143] Is such an image even thinkable without *presupposing* the air, without the air's invisible presence as the open placing of such emerging? Or, when Heidegger references "the sprouting of shoots, the emerging of the blossom" as images for emerging, can one envision such moments without also envisioning air – not air in the scientific sense of breathable gases, but in the inceptual sense of the open expanse of *world*?

So understood, the clearing – that is, being itself, understood in terms of φύσις, fire, etcetera – would be an emerging carried out in and through air: the very operation of such clearing, such emerging, would thus bear an essential connection to air.[144] Heidegger draws attention to this essential connection when, in GA 16, he describes the operation of clearing in terms of raising a boat's anchor from out of the water: "to raise [*lichten*] the anchor ... : to free it from the encompassing ocean floor and lift it into the free of water and air [*Freie des Wassers und der Luft*]."[145] The very process of clearing entails, on this iteration, a moving or drawing *into the air*, a *coming up for air*. Clearing entails the emerging into, or opening into, the open expanse of air: and the human, as (standing in) the clearing, would bear that connection no less.

There is a further sense in which the clearing is, at the very least, *like* air. As that opening emergence through which all beings come into the open, being, as the clearing, is the *nearest* to the human:[146] "Because φύσις does not hide itself, but is to the contrary the simple emerging and the open, it is the nearest of the near."[147] As the cleared being who withstands the open of the clearing, the human is *right up against* being, so to speak, pressed against it but largely unaware of that fact. In "The Letter on Humanism," Heidegger quite nearly

---

[143] GA 55: 137/104.
[144] On similar considerations with respect to Anaximenes' understanding of ἀήρ, see Sallis 1980, 151.
[145] GA 16: 630/220.   [146] GA 55: 103/78.   [147] GA 55: 141/106.

casts such nearness in terms of air: "Just as the openness of *spatial nearness* [*der räumlichen Nähe*] seen from the perspective of a particular thing exceeds all things near and far, so is being essentially broader than all beings, because it is the clearing itself."[148] The phrase "the openness of spatial nearness" can only be understood here as entailing the open of *air* – *not* air as the sciences conceive it (as an admixture of gases) but rather as the ur-phenomenon of the open expanse in which the human encounters things: For where does one ever encounter a *thing*, during the course of one's earthly sojourn, in the absence of such an airy open? In exactly the way that the air of a room makes possible the emergence of things while itself submerging behind them, drawing itself back into the inconspicuous, the clearing of being opens a play-space in which beings can show themselves while itself receding back into inconspicuousness: the two are functionally equivalent.[149]

In serving as the open of being's unfolding – in serving as the *Da* of *Sein* – the human itself, in a very real sense, would *be* this airy play-space, or at least would stand in its center in an exemplary manner. However, although this would hold true for the human *as such*, it is only the *thinker* who becomes *aware* of this airy open – it is only the thinker who *knows* he is drawn by the draft of this air. Nevertheless, such an atmosphere – that is, the atmosphere of *being* – is the very element of the human understood inceptually. All of this becomes clearer in *What Is Called Thinking?*, where Heidegger writes at some length regarding this *draft* (*Zug*) that belongs to thinking. Having argued that the human, rather than being naturally thoughtful, must indeed *learn* to think, Heidegger suggests that doing so requires that the human first "incline toward what addresses itself to thought,"[150] an address that, for the most part, goes unheeded. The reason for this is not (simply) ignorance or lack of attentiveness on the part of the human; rather, it is owing to the fact that what addresses itself to thought – namely the *thought-provoking*, or what the Heidegger of the Heraclitus lectures calls "the to-be-thought" – *withdraws*, concealing itself. However, as Heidegger argues, what withdraws, in its drawing away, is especially suited to drawing the human along with it in its withdrawal, pulling the human along with itself. One might be inclined to think of such a drawing along in terms of *water*, such as in the way that a wave or an undertow can pull one out to sea. However, Heidegger thinks of this withdrawing draw explicitly in terms of air:

---

[148] GA 9: 336–337/240; my emphasis. See also GA 9: 331/234.
[149] See GA 89: 16/13: "A clearing in the forest is still there, even when it's dark. Light presupposes clearing. There can only be brightness where something has been cleared or where something is free for the light. Darkening, taking away the light, does not encroach upon the clearing. The clearing is the presupposition for getting light and dark. It is the free, the open."
[150] GA 8: 19/17.

Once we are so related and drawn to what withdraws, we are drawing into what withdraws, into the enigmatic and therefore mutable nearness of its appeal. Whenever the human is properly drawing that way, he is thinking – even though he may still be far away from what withdraws, even though the withdrawal may remain as veiled as ever. All through his life and right into his death, Socrates did nothing else than place himself into the wind of this draft [*Zugwind dieser Zuges*] and maintain himself in it. This is why he is the purest thinker of the West. This is why he wrote nothing. For anyone who begins to write out of thoughtfulness must inevitably be like those people who flee any strong wind and seek refuge in the slipstream [*starkem Zugwind in den Windschatten*].[151]

To be a thinker in the genuine sense – to think thoughtfully – is to place oneself into the *draft* of the to-be-thought and to hold oneself within that draft,[152] to resist fleeing its force by taking refuge in the slipstream left by others. To *really* think, in other words, is to give oneself over to the full blast of "the crisp cool air of thinking" – that is, the air of being itself.

This connection to air is further emphasized by Heidegger a few pages later:

What withdraws from us draws us along by its very withdrawal, whether or not we become aware of it immediately, or at all. Once we are drawn into the withdrawal, we are – albeit in a way quite different from that of migratory birds – caught in the draft of what draws, attracts us by its withdrawal. And once we, being so attracted, are drawing toward what draws us, our essential being already bears the stamp of that "draft."[153]

The very being of the human is characterized – is influenced, shaped, or imprinted by – this draft, this air. Drawn along in the air of being, though not *quite* like birds in the sky, the human lives, we might say, in this draft, and so much so that it bears the stamp of that draft in its very essence. The human is thus *essentially* caught up in the draft of the (with)drawing of being.

Precisely because of the manner and extent to which the human is imprinted upon by this draft, the human *points* to it, calling it to mind:

As we are drawing toward what withdraws, we ourselves point toward it. We are who we are by pointing in that direction – not like an incidental adjunct but as follows: this "being in the draft of" is in itself an essential and therefore constant pointing toward what withdraws. To say "being in the draft of" is to say "pointing toward what withdraws." To the extent that the human is in this draft, he points toward what withdraws. As he is pointing that way, the human is the pointer.[154]

The human is the *pointer*, the *sign*, pointing toward what withdraws, and all of this because it is drawn into the wind, the *atmosphere,* the *air*, of being. As

---

[151] GA 8: 19–20/17.   [152] See Vallega-Neu 2018, 10.   [153] GA 8: 11/9.   [154] GA 8: 11/9.

Heidegger will go on to say, it is *only* because the human is drawn into this air that the human is *human*:

> The human is not first of all human and *then* also occasionally someone who points. No; drawn into what withdraws, drawing toward it and thus pointing into the withdraw, the human *first* is the human. His essential nature lies in being such a pointer. Something which in itself, by its essential nature, is a pointing, we call a sign. As he draws toward what withdraws, the human is a sign.[155]

It is thus on account of this draft – the air, the atmosphere, of being – that the human is what and as it is. In its very essence, the human bears witness to the draft, testifying to the air of being. The human is the sign of the atmosphere of being.

In the 1944 lecture course on Heraclitus's understanding of (the) Λόγος, Heidegger will explore another, related way in which air is foundational to human being. This comes to light during his analysis of the role of the ψυχή in its connection to λόγος, where the latter is understood as the gathering or "harvesting" proper to human existence – that is, the manner by which the human, by its very nature, gathers beings into coherence so as to experience them (in their being) as meaningful. (Indeed, this operation of gathering is so central to what it means to be human that Heidegger sometimes refers to the human simply as "The Gatherer.")[156] Heidegger begins by noting that the human is a living being, "a being that is determined by life."[157] This leads him into an inquiry into the nature of life, a nature that has everything to do with *nature*, so long as this is taken in the inceptual sense of φύσις. For the Greeks, according to Heidegger, both φύσις and ζωή are an "emerging-from-out-of-itself," an emerging that also "returns-back-into-itself":[158] "Emerging [e.g., of a living being] opens itself to the open, keeps it, in a certain sense, and maintains itself in the open and in this way contains the open within itself."[159] Said otherwise, what characterizes the life of a living being is the manner in which it remains open, in some manner, to the open clearing of being, and also returns to itself so as to experience, in some way, that open. In other words, to be alive is to stand, in some manner, in the opening clearing of being.

Such standing in the open of the open is characteristic, according to Heidegger, of the ψυχή, the "soul," which is to be understood as the very

---

[155] GA 8: 11/9.
[156] See GA 40: 132/191: "Human beings, as those who stand and act in *logos*, in gathering, are the gatherers." See also 71: 198/168: "[T]he original gatherer, the one that possesses together out of the gathered together, out of presencing lets everything emerge by way of coming to terms with things."
[157] GA 55: 280/212.   [158] GA 55: 280/212.   [159] GA 55: 280/212.

principle of life as such. As Heidegger notes, ψυχή principally means "a small puff of air [*Hauch*], a breath [*Atem*],"[160] though this meaning gets forgotten and left behind as the term undergoes its various metaphysical permutations. Against such metaphysical distortions, Heidegger wishes to reassert and maintain this connection between ψυχή and breathing, and thus the connection to air. However, he immediately criticizes the contemporary scientific understanding of such breathing. For Heidegger, breathing does not *merely* (*bloß*) refer to the physical act of drawing in and expelling air. Rather, breathing, as the "omnipresent, essential feature of the entire essence of what is alive," refers to the manner in which a living being "emerges into the open, and by emergingly going out into the open enters into its characteristic relationship with the open, thereby bringing the opening into that relationship and referring the open back to it."[161] Ψυχή, understood as breath, thus essentially consists "in the emerging self-opening into the open, an emerging that each time takes the open up and back into itself, and in this manner of taking upholds itself and abides in the open."[162] The drawing-in and drawing-out characteristic of the human – that is, its *breathing*, inceptually understood – is the manner by which the human gathers itself to the gathering of being.

There are two points to which to draw special attention here. First, it is important to note that Heidegger does not in any way deny that a living being's breathing entails the pulmonary action of pulling in and pushing out air. Rather, he claims that it does *not merely* (*nicht bloß*) consist of this physical act. Heidegger's critique here is not that scientific thinking is incorrect in claiming that all living beings ingest air, but that such thinking misses the more fundamental, ontological drawing in/drawing out (i.e., its opening into the open) that characterizes life as such. What this means, however, is that whenever Heidegger is discussing the manner in which a living being (i.e., a being with a ψυχή) emerges into the open and stands in (some) relation to that open, he is *also* conceiving such a being as *breathing* in the more mundane sense. In this way, the ingesting of air – and thus air itself – is implicit in Heidegger's (inceptual) understanding of *life*.

Secondly, and remarkably, Heidegger's discussion of life in the above passages implies that *all* living beings, and not only the human, abide in the open. Indeed, Heidegger goes on to make this point explicit:

> All that exists "lives" insofar as it is, and as something living, it is in some sense ensouled, though in a different manner in each case. This now means: the emergent relationship to the open and the openness of the open are

---

[160] GA 55: 280/212.   [161] GA 55: 281/212.   [162] GA 55: 281/212.

determined in different ways, all according to the kind of "living being," and also the other way around.[163]

All life, then, and not only human life, emerges into the open and relates to it, though always in different ways, and it is the idiosyncratic perimeters of such relating that determine the kind of life in each case. What distinguishes *human* life in particular is that its manner of abiding "conforms" to the open, *corresponds* to it: the human carries out a gathering, a drawing in and drawing out, that stands in a special, mirrored relation to that carried out by being itself. Simply put, the human stands in an originary concordance (*Entsprechen*) with being: its λόγος corresponds to – or, at least, *can* correspond to – the originary Λόγος of being itself.[164]

One could say, then, that the human stands within the *atmosphere* of the open to an enhanced degree – or, indeed, in a categorically different manner than any other living being. Although all living beings necessarily draw in and draw out within the open clearing of being, it is only the human who does so in such a way as to be *mindfully aware* of that fact; and to such awareness, to such *knowledge*, the ancient Greeks gave the name σοφία ("wisdom").[165] Such σοφία itself, as it turns out, must be understood, according to Heidegger, in its connection to air. This comes to light through Heidegger's analysis of Heraclitus's Fragment 112: "Thinking is the highest completeness, and wisdom is to say and to do the true according to the essence of things, hearkening to them [τὸ φρονεῖν ἀρετὴ μεγίστη, καὶ σοφίη ἀληθέα λέγειν καὶ ποιεῖν κατὰ φύσιν ἐπαΐοντας]."[166] During his analysis, Heidegger draws special attention to the final word of the fragment: "The last word is ἐπαΐοντας – ἀΐω means 'to waft [*wehen*],' 'to waft back-and-forth [*hin und her wehen*],' 'to draw-out toward something [*auf etwas hin ausholen*]' 'to draw-in [*einholen*].'"[167] While Heidegger's ultimate point here is to demonstrate that genuine knowledge consists of "listening attentively to *the* Λόγος" (i.e., to being), his elucidation of the word ἐπαΐοντας ("hearkening"), and his emphasis on its connection to ἀΐω (literally, "to breathe"), casts the entire fragment in terms of air. Genuine

---

[163] GA 55: 281/212. Capobianco reads this as referring to *all beings* (Capobianco 2022, 151). However, context makes it clear that Heidegger is referring to *living* beings, to beings "with" life, not to all beings whatsoever.

[164] GA 55: 281/213: "If the living being has a λόγος, then the drawing-out and drawing-in – i.e., the relationship to the open – is determined as 'harvesting' and 'gathering.' If that is so, then the living being is in the manner of the human: the 'harvesting' and 'gathering,' the λέγειν of the human, is ὁμολογεῖν. This emergent and thus unfolding being – i.e., the human – is open to the Λόγος."

[165] GA 55: 358/268; 370/276.   [166] GA 55: 359/269.   [167] GA 55: 370/376.

knowledge is the drawing in/drawing out, the wafting-along-in, the air of being: wisdom consists in *breathing in the air of being*.[168]

Heidegger then extends his argument to include *thinking*, claiming that "thinking is nothing other than the gathered gathering standing within knowing."[169] Thinking too, then, is to be understood as this drawing in/drawing out of the atmosphere of being, the kind of following-along-in-the-draft-of-being in which the superlatively thoughtful Socrates was so adept. Heidegger then connects such knowing, and such thinking, with *care*: "Thinking is the care of a concernful residing [*die Sorgfalt des sorgsamen Aufenthaltes*] within knowing. Thinking is care [*Sorge*]."[170]

As an aside, and in light of Heidegger's mention of *care*, one is inclined to ask: Could one read Heidegger's treatment of thinking and knowing, in their connection to ἄω (i.e., breathing/drawing in and out), back into his treatment of *care* within *Being and Time*? That is, could one find the invisible presence of air within the analysis of care therein? Heidegger never speaks about air directly within *Being and Time*, and yet one wonders if one can infer its invisible presence within his discussion of *spatiality* (*Räumlichkeit*). Differentiating *Dasein*'s spatiality from the sort of spatial locatedness that characterizes present-at-hand entities, Heidegger argues that "*Dasein* can *be* spatial only as care [*Sorge*]."[171] Foundationally structured by such care, *Dasein* "takes space in" and brings a space with itself, "making room for itself" and for the entities which it encounters: in other words, the human, owing to its fundamental constitution as care, *spaces* and *places* beings. (Later texts will suggest that such spacing is to be understood as the *clearing*, as the manner by which the clearing clears.)[172] Somewhat surprisingly, Heidegger then writes that it is "because *Dasein* is 'spiritual' [*geistig*], and only because of this, [that] it can be spatial in a way which remains essentially impossible for any extended corporeal Thing."[173] It is on account of its *spirit* (*Geist*), then, that the human clears a space of world in which beings appear and about which it can concern itself.

In this connection, one recalls that, in the "Myth of Cura" central to Heidegger's account of care, spirit (*spiritum*) is given to the human by Jupiter not long after Care has formed the human out of watery earth.[174] The Latin word *spiritum*, from which the English word "spirit" is directly derived, principally

---

[168] See GA 52: 55/48: "Does not this poem also show a connection between the 'blowing of the wind' and 'thinking'? Certainly. Yet the decisive question remains whether we conceive of thinking as a blowing, and blowing as a wind current, and the latter as a movement of air present before us, or whether we place such blowing, in its coming and going, carrying and bringing, into a relation to poetizing and thinking, and comprehend the wind and breath of air and thus 'spirit' too from out of this relation."

[169] GA 55: 371/277. [170] GA 55: 372/277. [171] GA 2: 486/336. [172] See GA 66: 102/85.
[173] GA 2: 487/336. [174] GA 2: 262/184.

means "breath" or "air," a signification that is also present in the German *Geist*. It is *breath* and *air* that Jupiter gives to the human, and it is the air, this *spirit*, that makes *Dasein*'s sojourn in the open clearing of the world possible. It is on account of such spirit that *Dasein* clears a space – the very space of its world – in which to carry out its existence.

Turning back now to the 1944 Heraclitus lectures we turn to a passage in which Heidegger focuses on the foundational role that air plays within the operation of the drawing-in/drawing-out characteristic of the human ψυχή:

> But what do we encounter as the main characteristic of ψυχή according to the meaning of the word? The word means puff, breath, the breath of life [*der Hauch, der Atem, der Odem*]. Is it merely a coincidence that, when the soul slips away, we say that the breath of life has expired and the light of life has been extinguished? Why is it that we consider both "breath" and "light" as having the same relation to the fundamental characteristic of the living thing? Light is the lightening – it is that which lightens and opens, and which, as the bright, holds open. Breath, grasped broadly and properly enough as not being limited to air, is the drawing-in and drawing-out, the emerging into the open and the pulling back in of the open. In fact, if we think of air as ether, then "air" and "light" coincide. However, for our belated thinking they only coincide because they are one in their concealed essence: they are one and the same with "life" and φύσις.[175]

The clearing itself, then, is to be understood in its essential unity with the inceptual understanding of breath: the clearing is the lightening, airy, ether-like opening of being.[176] Properly grasped, air "coincides" with "light" understood as the lightening of the clearing: thus, when one hears the word "clearing" in Heidegger's thought, one must also think of *air*, inceptually grasped.

In order to see this a bit more concretely, one might turn to one additional passage in the Heraclitus lectures, back in the 1943 course on φύσις. There, Heidegger provides a certain remarkable description of the clearing unfolding of being, a *scene* of sorts in which one can perhaps see – insofar as one can ever *see* – the role that air plays in such a clearing. During a discussion of the inceptual understanding of animality (in distinction to the modern scientific account), Heidegger offers the following:

> we need only to take a few steps away from the vague and indeterminate modern conception of the bird in order to experience and recognize the bird as the Greeks did: namely, as the animal through whose swaying and hovering [*Anschweben*] the free dimension of the open unfolds, and through whose

---

[175] GA 55: 300/226.

[176] See also GA 52: 121/103: "These dreams that sustain art are terrifying, yet divine. Terrifying, because they arise out of humankind like something foreign and disconcerting and yet as one's ownmost, filling the ether (the air) in which humankind finds its essence."

singing the tidings the call and the enchantment unfold, so that its bird-essence whiles away and disperses in the open.[177]

As I have written about elsewhere, this scene is remarkable for several reasons, not the least of which is the manner in which it shows the otherwise wordless *animal* capable of pointing to, or allowing to unfold, the clearing of being. However, what is of interest presently is the way in which this scene of the opening clearing of being demonstrates the implicit role of air therein. For can one picture birds "swaying" and "hovering" without thereby picturing air? Can one imagine "the free dimension of the open" without (thereby) imaging air? Is it not the case that air is the very medium, the very *element*, of this open clearing in which the bird hovers?

However, it is precisely the "vague and indeterminate" understanding of things that prevails in the contemporary era; as a result, the human has more and more forgotten about the air of the clearing precisely as it learns more about air scientifically understood.[178] Such a transition has had dire consequences for the human as it sinks deeper and deeper into a forgetfulness of being. Heidegger speaks to this point in his Bremen lectures from 1949, during his famous discussion of the jug. Having just argued that, properly understood, it is the *emptiness* of the jug – that is, the vacuous space between the curved boundaries of its surface, or what Heidegger will call "this nothing in the jug [*dieses Nichts am Krug*]" – that allows the jug to hold wine or water and thus *be* what it is (namely a vessel for holding and outpouring), Heidegger ventriloquizes the following scientific rebuttal: "The physical sciences assure us that the jug is filled with air and with all that constitutes the compound mixture of air."[179] According to this view, when one pours a liquid into a jug, one does not pour it into an *emptiness*. Rather, the scientist would tell us that "if we pour wine into the jug we merely force out the air that already fills the jug and replace it with a fluid."[180]

The contemporary scientific account of air thus leads the human to overlook the emptiness, or the *nothing*, of the jug. In so doing, the human is compelled to think about air as a representational object, as the "compound mixture" of chemicals. Such a view, in overlooking the *nothing* at the heart of the jug in favor of a projected ontological framework, loses touch with *nothingness* itself – that is, it loses sight of the clearing opening of being that, while serving as the site in which things appear, is itself no *thing*, is itself *nothing*. The scientific account of air is thus precisely what leads to the human's overlooking of being itself: air understood as a chemical compound obscures the human's vision of the air of the clearing of being.

---

[177] GA 55: 95/72.   [178] See GA 5: 291/113.   [179] GA 79: 8/8.   [180] GA 79: 8/8.

What is required, then, is a thoughtful reawakening of the inceptual meaning of air understood as the clearing of being itself. In his "Memorial Address" from 1955, Heidegger will call such thoughtful reawakening "meditative thinking," where this is to be understood as the thoughtful attending to the being of beings, an attending that necessarily entails a movement away from the calculative thinking characteristic of the present age. Such meditative thinking is depicted there as a movement up into the *ether*, up into the "free air [*freie Luft*] of the high heavens."[181] Just as the clearing itself should be understood as a movement from the concealment of deep water up into the light of day, so too should meditative thinking be understood as a movement up from the earth into the heavenly air above. Only through such an ascent into the air of thinking can the human save itself from the danger that presses upon it:

> What great danger then might move upon us? Then there might go hand in hand with the greatest ingenuity in calculative planning and inventing indifference toward meditative thinking, total thoughtlessness. And then? Then the human would have denied and thrown away his own special nature – that he is a meditative being. Therefore, the issue is the saving of the human's essential nature. Therefore, the issue is keeping meditative thinking alive.[182]

Entering into the atmosphere of being through meditative thinking is thus essential to the human's grasp of its own essence. Before the human can become its proper self, it must learn how to breathe the air of being.

Cut off from the crisp cool air of thinking, the contemporary human is out of its proper atmosphere, out of its proper element, and thus outside of its proper essence. One could say, then, that the human of the present era is that entity who is still *holding its breath*, waiting to come up for air and breathe in the air of being, waiting to be carried away by its draft. Once it catches its breath, drawing the air of being into itself, the human, as Heidegger writes in "What Are Poets For" (from 1946), will finally be able to harness that air and *sing forth* the meaning of being, thus entering into its proper essence:

> To sing, truly to say worldly existence, to say out of the haleness of the whole pure draft and to say only this, means: to belong to the precinct of beings themselves. This precinct, as the very nature of language, is Being itself. To sing the song means to be present in what is present itself. It means: *Dasein*.[183]

---

[181] GA 16: 521/48.   [182] GA 16: 582–583/56.   [183] GA 5: 316/138.

4 Fire: The Sufferer

The human – so the story goes – is the only mortal being capable of making *fire*. The story, of course, is the story of Prometheus, the transgressive Titan who stole fire from the citadel of the gods and brought it to humans, thereby condemning himself to an eternity of suffering. There are many different iterations of this story, the simplest and most concise of which is offered by Sappho from the sixth century BCE (as reported by Virgil in his *Eclogues*): "After creating the human, Prometheus is said to have stolen fire and revealed [*indicavit*] it to them."[184] In the *Protagoras* of Plato – that thinker who, according to Heidegger, initiated the representational/technological thinking characteristic of the modern age[185] – one finds a more expansive and complicated account:

> There once was a time when the gods existed but mortal races did not. When the time came for their appointed genesis, the gods molded them inside the earth, blending together earth and fire and various compounds of earth and fire. When they were ready to bring them to light [πρὸς φῶς] the gods put Prometheus and Epimetheus in charge of decking them out and assigning to each its appropriate powers and abilities.[186]

Taking over the actual task of meting out capacities, Prometheus's brother Epimetheus bequeathed to all living things the abilities that would come to characterize them (i.e., flight to birds, thick skin to cows, prodigious procreative power to rabbits, etc.). However, because

> Epimetheus was not very wise, he absentmindedly used up all the powers and abilities on the nonreasoning animals [τὰ ἄλογα]; he was left with the human race, completely unequipped. While he was floundering about at a loss, Prometheus arrived to inspect the distribution and saw that while the other animals were well provided with everything, the human race was naked, unshod, unbedded, and unarmed, and it was already the day on which all of them, human beings included, were destined to emerge from the earth into the light [ἐκ γῆς εἰς φῶς]. It was then that Prometheus, desperate to find some means of survival for the human race, stole from Hephaestus and Athena wisdom in the practical arts together with fire (without which this kind of wisdom is effectively useless) and gave them outright to the human race.[187]

Unlike in Sappho's account, the Prometheus of Plato's *Protagoras* does not *make* the human: rather, the gods, having already created mortal beings – indeed, having created them out of an admixture of earth and fire – gave those beings over to Prometheus and his brother so that they might equip them with

---

[184] Sappho, Fragment 207. [185] See, for example, GA 79: 7/7; GA 65: 184/144.
[186] *Prot.* 320d.   [187] *Prot.* 321c–d.

the abilities that would come to be characteristic of them. However, although Prometheus does not make the human in this telling, he nonetheless makes the human *human* – that is, he gives to the human that which makes the human distinct from all of the other animals, namely fire and the technics that become possible with it.[188] This telling of the story positions the human with respect to other living beings by proposing that the human is essentially *technological*, that it has τέχνη as part of its very being: to be human is to have – and to *have* to have – the technological means by which to engage and interact with the earthworld. In this way fire would be implicit in all human activity, at least so far as that activity is essentially enabled by, or expressive of, or always reliant upon, τέχνη.[189]

Although much of Heidegger's critical engagement with technology could be seen as addressing, at least indirectly, the Promethean legacy that defines the human as essentially technological, there is only one passage within his entire corpus where he addresses the myth itself at length. The passage occurs within the book *Mindfulness* (1938–1939) and serves as the first entry of Part VII of the book, entitled "Being and the Human." The paragraph in which the reference to Prometheus occurs itself has the heading "Being and the Human," as if to emphasize that it is this relationship that is at stake in what follows:

> If beyng inceptually came to word as φύσις, and if φύσις and φάος say the Same in its multiplicity – namely, emerging clearing within the interrelation of opening and incandescence – then the inceptual metaphysical experience of the human as the living being who has λόγος entails at the same time the experience of the human as the being [*Wesens*] that "has" the glow, the fire – the sole being [*Wesen*] who can make "fire." In this case "fire" is not only, as conflagration and brightness, a "means" of τέχνη ... but is rather, as the clearing – ἀλήθεια – the ground of τέχνη. Thus, Prometheus did not first bring "fire" to "the human" as an addition; rather, the human became the human only through this action of the Titan. ... And so, from the very inception, the history of the human and the possibility of machination as the groundlessness of the clearing are decided in τέχνη.[190]

Even more so than the account given in Plato' *Protagoras*, Heidegger's (re)telling emphasizes the way in which the human *becomes* human – that is, attains its every essence – through Prometheus's bestowal of fire: however, the fire in question in Heidegger's telling is of a different sort than that seemingly meant in the Platonic account. Heidegger's (re)telling involves a duplication, a kind of *doubling*, of

---

[188] In the Platonic version, Zeus, via Hermes, later sends "justice and a sense of shame" to humans (*Prot.* 322c).
[189] Stiegler 1998, 194.   [190] GA 66: 135/115.

fire.[191] On the one hand, there is the fire of technicity understood as means or instrument, the fire that, for example, makes welding and melting possible. On the other hand, and more fundamentally, there is the fire of ἀλήθεια, the fire of the clearing – that is, there is the fire of being itself understood as unconcealment.[192] This fire serves as the very ground of the fire of technicity, and it is *this* fire – the fire of the clearing of being – that was brought to the human "through the action of the Titan" and that distinguishes the human as the human. The human thus "makes" fire not only with sticks and friction, or with butane lighters and lightbulbs, but by virtue of its very *being* – by virtue, that is, of serving as the site (i.e., the *Da*) of the lightening clearing of being.

The human is thus the sole being who, by virtue of having been gifted this foundational fire, stands openly in the open clearing of being. And yet, as the end of the above passage suggests, this more fundamental fire has been decided against, has been *forgotten*, in favor of the other fire, the fire of technicity. Such forgetting, for Heidegger, is emblematic of the contemporary age, an age more and more characterized by the human's fascination with technology, and, indeed, it is that fascination that continues to obscure the human's genuine relationship to being.[193] By perceiving itself more and more as the master of beings, capable of producing and manipulating them at will and without limit, the human, (mis)taking *itself* for the very ground of beings – that is, as the very *being* of beings – loses sight of its own essential relation to being, its essential *Other* through whom its own character is determined.

As Heidegger suggests in his 1944 lectures on Heraclitus, this presumed posture of technological mastery can itself be understood in terms of fire:

> there ignites a burning and scorching flame [*eine brennende und versengende Lohe*] within the emerging originary self-lightening clearing of the human essence, a blaze [*jenes Brennende*] that burns and yearns to measure these paths autonomously and selfishly, a measuring that is always merely a mismeasuring and, indeed, a presumptuous one (i.e., ὕβρις).[194]

As I have argued elsewhere, it is this burning fire belonging to the human's hubristic usurping of being that threatens to overshadow the human's relation to being, and therefore the human's cognizance of the more originary fire that burns at (and as) its essence.[195] Heidegger references this situation in the following passage from *Contributions to Philosophy* (1936–1938), a text that bears a special affinity with *Mindfulness*:

---

[191] The Platonic account also contains a doubling, though of a different sort. Twice within the passage, "the light of day" is referenced: the sun is thus the second, unspoken fire that operates in the background of the story.
[192] See GA 65: 431/340.   [193] GA 66: 173–174/151–152.   [194] GA 55: 392/290.
[195] See Ewegen 2021.

> The sudden extinguishing of the great fire [i.e., the fire of beyng] – this leaves behind something which is neither day nor night, which no one grasps, and in which humans, having come to the end, still bustle about so as to benumb themselves with the products of their machinations.[196]

Living in a kind of twilight state – a state, one might suppose, in which even the fire of the sun and the stars has been forgotten in favor of the "fire" of electric light[197] – the human loses contact with that luminant glow that serves as the very core of (its) being.[198]

As the rest of Heidegger's account in *Mindfulness* (and elsewhere) makes clear, the task of the human is one of *retrieving* – or, one might say, *rekindling*[199] – this more originary sense of fire:

> In that case, the first inception of the *history* of the human would have to retrieve its un-unfolded inceptuality entirely from out of the en-saying of the other beginning. In that case, the relation of man's ownmost to be-ing and the sway of being itself would have to be thought more inceptually than metaphysics had been hitherto capable of doing with respect to its own beginning.[200]

Engulfed by the fire of technicity, and awash in the artificial light of the contemporary age, the human must work to retrieve the inceptual meaning of being (as clearing). Heidegger speaks again of this retrieval later on in *Mindfulness*:

> However, in the meantime something else comes to pass occasionally, and the resolute individuals see the glowing hidden hearth-fire of all beings and intimate what is futural to their guardians, which does not come like a romantic dream only after this present epoch, but has already come and has gifted be-ing to the historical recollection as refusal and has allowed man to know what is the 'other' to his own self.[201]

The path beyond the travails of the contemporary obsession with technicity, and the widespread devastation to which it has led, was thus gifted to the human long ago: indeed, one could understand it as the *original gift*, the gift of the insurgence of being (i.e., *Es Gibt*) itself, a gift that has, with some notable

---

[196] GA 66: 262/207.
[197] See GA 55: 142/108: "The human being then fashions a light for himself. As a result of such fashioning, the modern metropolis, even before the war, had already turned night into day by means of a technology of illumination, so that neither the sky nor the lights that belong to it can be seen. As a result of this lighting technology, brightness itself has become an object that can be produced. Brightness, in the sense of the inconspicuous in all shining, has lost its essence. However, brightness, in the sense of the pellucidity of the light, is grounded in the fact that, above all else, clearing and emergence (i.e., φύσις) unfold."
[198] See also GA 5: 326/245.   [199] GA 66: 243/214.   [200] GA 66: 135/115.
[201] GA 66: 277/245.

exceptions, given itself heretofore only in its refusal and withdrawal. Thus, the human can only move *forward* through the fires of technicity by moving *back* toward that which has already been gifted to the human but which, owing to the self-concealing character of that gift, the human has forgotten; however, because such a retrieval has yet to be carried out, and because it opens up heretofore unexhausted possibilities, one must understand it as a *futural* gesture, as something *yet* to come, as preparation for something long since *presented* that has yet to become present: an *unopened gift*.

Much of Heidegger's thought – and arguably *all* of it – focuses itself on the task of bringing the human (back) to this inceptual fire, of thinking beyond technicity and retrieving the more originary fire that belongs to the human and constitutes its being. Indeed, this gesture of retrieval comes to typify, for Heidegger, the proper *work* of the human, a work the carrying out of which would transform the human into its proper being as *Da-sein*. In one of his Black Notebooks (1931–1938), Heidegger speaks about this work in the following way:

> A new era is arising in which all authorities and institutions, all endeavors and standards, will be fused together – and everything depends on our creating [*schaffen*] the correct original fire and the thoroughly genuine metal for the new amalgam and on our making it fluid in the coming *Dasein*. This fire is the "truth" in the original essence of truth, and the glowing, consuming, purifying flame of this fire is questioning. But the metal, the genuineness of the earth, is beyng.[202]

One can hear unmistakable Promethean undertones in this passage. Not at all unlike the manner in which the gods, according to the Prometheus myth, made the human by "blending together earth and fire and various compounds of earth and fire," the human of the contemporary era must *create* the *Dasein* to come,[203] must *build* it out of fire and earth. In this way, the human must serve as its own Prometheus, bequeathing to itself the alethic fire of being so that it might (finally) become the *Dasein* it is fated to become.

That being said, it is important to note that such creating does not take place as the implementing of certain techniques or the employing of certain technologies so as to bring about some new entity, for such a strategy would merely reinforce the problematic and willful logic of technological thinking that Heidegger seeks to overcome. Rather, this creating takes place as the fervent *questioning* in the face of being, a questioning after the *meaning* of being, for "only the cool boldness of thinking and the dark errancy of questioning lend ardor and light to the fire of beyng."[204] Through such questioning – which

---

[202] GA 94: 178/130; trans. modified.   [203] See GA 94: 282/278.   [204] GA 65: 430/340.

Heidegger elsewhere describes as the highest action of which the human is capable[205] – the human continues to kindle the fire of this (most) originary being, thereby enkindling the fire of its own essence.

Somewhat paradoxically, this project of (re)kindling the original fire of being entails a certain sensitivity for what at first blush appears to be the very opposite of fire, namely the *dark*. Heidegger says as much in his *Contributions to Philosophy*:

> Beyng: the hearth-fire in the midst of the lodging of the gods. . . . How to find beyng? Must we light a fire in order to find the fire, or must we not rather reconcile ourselves to guarding [*behüten*] over the night first? Thereby the false days of everydayness might be resisted. The most false of those days are the ones that profess to know and to possess even the night when they illumine and thus eliminate it with their borrowed light.[206]

Precisely as a way to avoid the artificial fires of technicity, the human must reconcile itself to the night, must experience and *guard* that darkness, for it is in this darkness that the human (first) feels the abandonment of being, thereby becoming *aware* of being (in its withdrawal).[207] As Heidegger elsewhere makes clear, attending to the night amounts to cultivating a sensitivity toward the *concealment* that serves as the intimate counterpart to being's unconcealment, the λήθη that serves as the heart of ἀλήθεια. What matters is that the human comes to experience something of the insoluble intimacy of submergence and emergence, concealment and unconcealment, that characterizes the truth of being.[208] In his Heraclitus lectures from 1943, where he draws a certain equivalency between the early Greek understanding of being and fire (i.e., πῦρ), Heidegger offers the following regarding such intimacy:

> Fire flames and is, in enflaming, the excising separation between the light and the dark: enflaming joins the light and the dark against, and into, one another. In enflaming, there occurs something that the eye grasps in a glimpse, something instantaneous and singular, which decisively excises the bright from the dark. The instantaneity of enflaming makes room for appearance over against the region of vanishing. In particular, the instantaneity of enflaming lightens the region of all indicating and showing, but also lightens, at the same time, the region of directionlessness, rudderlessness, and absolute opacity. This flaming/excising essence that first bears light and dark toward one another and yokes them together is the defining essence of fire – an essence that no chemistry could ever grasp, because it must destroy this essence in advance in order to then make it comprehensible to itself.[209]

---

[205] GA 66: 156/134. [206] GA 65: 487/383. [207] See GA 65: 486/383. [208] GA 71: 13/7.
[209] GA 55: 161/122. On all of this, see Mitchell 2015, 153–154.

It is thus precisely by attending to the true character of the fire (of being) that the human comes into contact with the concealment at the dark heart of being, a character that the fake fires of technicity threaten to obscure through their ersatz illumination.

Although the poet and the thinker prove to be especially adept at attending to being in this way, rekindling the human's awareness of it,[210] such attending is, strictly speaking, the proper work of the human as such.[211] Indeed as Heidegger makes clear elsewhere, it is simply synonymous with the *care* that serves as the fundamental constitution of the human understood as *Dasein*:

> Da-sein and human being are essentially related, inasmuch as Da-sein signifies the ground of the possibility of future human being, and humans are futural by accepting to be the "there," provided they understand themselves as the stewards of the truth of beyng. This stewardship is indicated by the term "care."[212]

Through embracing and carrying out the care by means of which it attends to the alethic truth of being, the human enters into its own proper essence, fulfilling its destined role as the steward of being. Heidegger makes this point in one of his Black Notebooks in the following rhetorical way: "Who is the future human being … ? Answer: the steward of the stillness of the passing by of the last god – the grounding preserver of the truth of beyng."[213] The human is – or someday will be – the preserver of the alethic truth, the unconcealment, of being.

Interestingly, in a different Black Notebook, Heidegger indicates an essential connection between the caring stewardship proper to the human and the Titan Prometheus:

> To be there [*da-sein*] in fundamentally different realms of beyng, indeed ones no longer even comparable in their differences, and at the same time to grant to those who are oblivious a full right to their obliviousness – *Da-sein* as "care" (προ-μηθεῖσθαι ["forethought"]).[214]

Heidegger then elaborates upon the nature of this Promethean care central to *Dasein*'s being:

> But care as care over fire qua light and clearing (φάος – φύσις ["light – nature"]) – the care of beyng – (being and time).[215]

Care, which is the very ground of *Dasein*'s being, is thus essentially Promethean insofar as this is understood as the care over the *fiery* clearing of being of which

---

[210] GA 4: 68/90.
[211] Such rekindling (*Entfachen*) is also, as he makes clear in *Being and Time*, the purpose of his *own* work. See GA 2: 577/487.
[212] GA 65: 297/234. [213] GA 94: 334/243. [214] GA 96: 170/134. [215] GA 96: 170/134.

only the human is capable. Such care amounts, for Heidegger, to a stewardship of the truth of being whereby the human shelters both the clearing of (the truth) of being *and* the concealment that serves as the abyssal ground of that clearing.[216] It is through such Promethean stewardship, such care, that the human enters into its proper essence.

At the end of the above passage, Heidegger writes "being and time" as a way to further elucidate the "care over fire as light and clearing" that constitutes the human's solicitude toward being. It is not clear whether these two words, "*Sein und Zeit*," are meant to refer the interrelated phenomena of being and time as an index for the care for being, or to the title of Heidegger's book that bears that name. If the former – but even, to some extent, if the later, since it is precisely the relationship between being and time that is foremost explored within that book – Heidegger here invites us to consider the possibility that the care elucidated in *Being and Time* is to be understood as having an essentially *Promethean* character, and is thus, in some manner, to be understood in terms of fire.[217]

Along these lines, one thinks of that passage within *Being and Time*, already analyzed in Section 1, where Heidegger draws a certain equivalency between the human and the clearing that opens a time-space for beings in which to show themselves:

> When we talk in an ontically figurative way of the *lumen naturale* in the human, we have in mind nothing other than the existential-ontological structure of this entity, that it is in such a way as to be its "there." To say that it is "illuminated" [*erleuchtet*] means that as Being-in-the-world it is cleared [*gelichtet*] in itself, not through any other entity, but in such a way that it is itself the clearing. Only for an entity which is existentially cleared in this way does that which is present-at-hand become accessible in the light or hidden in the dark. By its very nature, *Dasein* brings its "there" along with it.[218]

On this account, the human "is" the clearing of being's unfolding, and is itself cleared. To the word "cleared" Heidegger later annotates the following: "*Aletheia* – openness-clearing, light, shining." The human is that being who stands within the truth of being understood as the open, bright shining of being, a shining that unfolds from out of the concealment implicit in truth understood as ἀ-λήθεια. The human, as the clearing, stands within the interplay of concealment and unconcealment, and brings this interplay along with (and as) itself.

What if one were to read this passage in light of Heidegger's later thinking of fire? For example, what if one were to read this passage in light of what

---
[216] GA 65: 297/235.
[217] On a different take on the "promethean" character of Heidegger's thought, see Miller 1996.
[218] GA 2: 177/125.

Heidegger says in his 1943 lectures on Heraclitus, where he draws a conceptual equivalence between φύσις, ἀλήθεια, and πῦρ ("fire")?[219] Could one not then understand this passage from *Being and Time* as suggesting that *Dasein*, *as* the cleared *Da* of *Sein*, always brings (its) *fire* (i.e., its *lumen naturale*) along with itself, that it always opens up its world by means of this originary fire, a fire that flickers on the threshold of light and dark? Would not the very word "*Dasein*" then, in this way, equally always denote fire, insofar as it always referred to the foundationally fiery clearing that characterizes its caring structure?

If so, one could (re)turn one final time to the "Myth of Cura" in *Being and Time*, now reading that myth as a *reinscription* of the Prometheus story; only, on Heidegger's telling, fire would not be *stolen* from the gods, but would rather be freely imparted to the human by its creator, by Care (or, perhaps, by Jupiter, who gives the human spirit), and would consist of nothing other than such care. Like the gods in the myth of Prometheus, Care would form the human out of earth and fire, insofar as the latter is understood by Heidegger as nothing other than the care of beyng itself.

In light of all of this, one wonders: Is the human, like Prometheus, fated to an eternity of *suffering*?[220] Is the Promethean care that characterizes the human *transgressive* – or *ecstatic* – such that the human, in exhibiting and "making use" of such care, must pay some inexhaustible penalty for it? Could this be why, for Heidegger, the *exposure* to the truth of beyng destined to the futural human comes to be characterized by great *suffering* – not the sort of ontic suffering with which all-too-many humans in the present techno-focused epoch are familiar, but an *originary* and *creative* suffering deeper and more foundational than any bodily or emotional suffering? For, according to Heidegger, it is

> only in such suffering [that] a destiny [can] take hold of us, a destiny that never simply lies present before us, but that is a sending – that is, is sent to us – and in such a way that it sends us toward our vocation, granted that we ourselves truly send ourselves into it, and know of what is fittingly sent, and, in knowing it, will it.[221]

So understood, suffering would be the very *name* for how the human, as Da-sein, receives the gift given to it by being, a suffering by means of which it enters into its own proper vocation, its own proper being. Suffering would be *how* the human occupies its role as the steward of being.

As would be expected, it is, according to Heidegger, the poets and the thinkers who are most capable of this supreme suffering and who come to typify it: for it is they who must initially leap away from the fires of modernity

---

[219] GA 55: 326/244.   [220] See Miller 1996, 202.   [221] GA 39: 176/160.

and into the inceptual fire of beyng.²²² Speaking specifically of *thinkers* at one point in his Bremen lectures, Heidegger writes that

> what the thinker says of being is not his opinion. What is said is the echo speaking through him of the claim that essences as beyng itself in that It brings itself to language. To be an echo is more difficult and more rare than to have opinions and to represent standpoints. To be an echo is the suffering of thinking.²²³

The poets and the thinkers, in echoing the call of being, carry out and exemplify their heightened ability to suffer. However, through this acute suffering, and in serving as the echo of beyng, the poets and thinkers help usher the human as such into its own proper suffering. As he puts it in his lecture on Hölderlin's "Germania,"

> In such strife, an inhering within the middle of being, between gods and humans, is fought for and attained and, at the same time, suffered. Beyng as destiny is only where such suffering attunes our passion and becomes the fundamental attunement of *Dasein*.²²⁴

The suffering of being is thus to become the foundational comportment of the human, a suffering that transforms the very humanity of the human. The human must move beyond the counterfeit suffering of the contemporary era – a suffering it ignores and attempts to palliate by means of modern technologies²²⁵ – and move into a truer, more genuine suffering, the suffering of beyng itself. So understood, the human, for Heidegger, is the one who does not yet suffer *enough*, who, in coming to care for the beyng long ago gifted to it, will one day enter into deeper, more authentic suffering.

In this way, the human, like Prometheus, is *destined* to suffer, and suffering will, for the *Dasein* to come, prove to be its most proper element:

> What is needed now is the great inversion, one beyond all "revaluation of values," an inversion in which beings are not grounded on the human being, but humanness on beyng. That, however, requires a higher power of creating and questioning and at the same time a deeper readiness for suffering [*Leiden*] and enduring in the entirety of a complete transformation of the relations to beings and to beyng.²²⁶

Conclusion: The Shepherd

In the preceding sections, we have seen the ways in which the existence of the human remains pervaded by the so-called elements, by earth, water, air, and fire,

---

²²² See GA 65: 6/8. ²²³ GA 79: 66/62. ²²⁴ GA 39: 274/249. ²²⁵ See GA 5: 274/204.
²²⁶ GA 65: 184/145.

all of which play essential parts within the existential structure of the human. Within Heidegger's thought, the elements are no longer conceived as material components of an entity understood in terms of modern (or even Aristotelian) physics, but as *ontological* elements essential to the very being of the human. In other words, these elements become, through Heidegger's thinking, another way of articulating *how* the human relates to the proper element of its being – that is, being itself – and thereby earns the determinant character of its *own* being. To be human is to walk on the earth amongst the things of the earth, to be utterly immersed within the fluidity of language, to breathe the air of the clearing of being, and to stand within the radiant glow of the fire of that clearing.

For Heidegger, this elemental language is more than metaphorical: it is *phenomenological*. A metaphor can only operate in relation to a prior, more primitive experience whose shape and contours it attempts to explain by means of some other experience. But, for Heidegger, the elements of earth, water, air, and fire refer precisely to that primitive, inceptual experience of being human: they are a means of describing the most basic, foundational element to human being, namely being itself. The fact that such descriptions have a largely *poetic* character does not mean that they stray from the truth; to the contrary, such poetic language *ensures*, for Heidegger, the disclosive power of such descriptions. As he puts it in his *Basic Problems of Phenomenology* (1927), "Poetry, creative literature, is nothing but the elementary emergence into words [*elementare Zum-Wort-kommen*], the becoming-uncovered of existence as being-in-the-world. For the others who before it were blind, the world first becomes visible by what is thus spoken."[227] The language of the elements that Heidegger employs thus serves as an enhanced way to bring the primeval role of being within human life to light.

As seen in the preceding study, the path by means of which the human journeys into its ownmost essence entails cultivating an awareness, a *mindfulness*, of these elements and the manner in which they bear upon being and, thus, upon *human* being. One sees further evidence of this in the following passage from one of Heidegger's Black Notebooks:

> Once more: the world is in reconstruction toward itself. We are again approaching the truth and its essentiality – we are becoming mindful of everything the truth requires to take it up and to take a stand within it – to become ones who are indigenous, who stand on native soil [*boden-ständig zu werden*]. The one who can be indigenous is the one who derives from native soil, is nourished by it, stands on it – this is the original – that is what often vibrates in me through body and disposition – as if I went over the fields guiding a plow, or over lonely field-paths amid ripening grain, through winds

---
[227] GA 24: 244/171.

and fog, sunshine and snow, paths which kept mother's blood, and that of her ancestors, circulating and pulsing.[228]

To truly belong to the world is to come from the *earth* (*aus Boden herkommend*), to be nourished by it. But it is also to walk on that earth through the other elements, through "wind and fog, sunshine and snow." To be human in the fullest sense, for Heidegger, is to wander among the elements of earth, water, air, and fire, to feel them vibrating (*schwingt*) within one's body and existential dis*position* (*Stimmung*). In other words, to be genuinely human is to recognize the extent to which these elements, as expressions of being itself, *pervade* one's very essence. Such mindful recognition entails, for example, becoming aware of

> the mature rest of the mountains, the concentrated illumination of the meadows, the silent flight of the falcon, the bright cloud in the immense sky – that wherein the great stillness of the remotest proximity of beyng has already announced itself.[229]

Here, the earth of the mountain, the fire that lights the meadow, the air that holds the falcon aloft, and the water that comprises the cloud, all carry the call of beyng's announcement, a call to which the mindful human is attentive.[230] All four elements play their role here, serving as an axis in terms of which the mindful human might mark the perimeters of its worldly sojourn.

Knowing these elements would be to know the world as the unfolding clearing of being *and* to know the role that the human plays therein: for it is *this* human – the human who discerns the elements of being in their elementality – who comes to know its proper role as the *shepherd* of being, a shepherd who, as Heidegger writes,

> knows nothing other than the stony path and the source, the alpine meadows and the clouds, the sun, and the storm.[231]

To know these elements, then, would be to know being and *thus* the human being: it would be to fully grasp, as human, the polyvalent nature of one's most pervasive and foundational element.

---

[228] GA 94: 38/29.   [229] GA 94: 305/223.
[230] To this description, Heidegger adds a poem entitled "The Fountainhead at Stübenwasen," the first lines of which make the role of water more explicit: "A pure streaming from the concealed | base of the mountain" (GA 94: 305/223).
[231] GA 39: 52/51. See also GA 94: 324/236: "Where and how do we preserve the open and never-dying fire of the most concealed intimacy? A grey-white cloud puff is dissipating into the blue sky of a windy summer day on solitary mountains."

References

Texts of Heidegger's Cited

The German volumes of Heidegger's *Gesamtausgabe* are cited in each case, followed by the corresponding English translations (when available). All editions from the *Gesamtausgabe* are published by Vittorio Klostermann, Frankfurt.

GA 2. *Sein und Zeit*. 1977. Edited by Friedrich Wilhelm von Herrmann. *Being and Time*. 1996. Translated by Joan Stambaugh. Albany: State University of New York Press.

GA 4. *Erläuterungen zu Hölderlins Dichtung*. 1981. Edited by Friedrich-Wilhelm von Herrmann. *Elucidations of Hölderlin's Poetry*. 2000. Translated by Keith Hoeller. Amherst, NY: Humanity Books.

GA 5. *Holzwege*. 1977. Edited by Friedrich-Wilhelm von Hermann. *Off the Beaten Track*. 2002. Translated by Julian Young and Kenneth Haynes. Cambridge: Cambridge University Press.

Poetry, Language, Thought. 1971. Translated by Albert Hoftstadter. New York: Harper and Row.

GA 7. *Vorträge und Aufsätze*. 2000. Edited by Friedrich-Wilhelm von Herrmann. *Poetry, Language, Thought*. 1971. Translated by Albert Hoftstadter. New York: Harper and Row.

GA 8. *Was heißt Denken?* 2002. Edited by Paola-Ludovika Coriando. *What Is Called Thinking?* 1968. Translated by J. Glenn Gray. New York: Harper and Row.

GA 9. *Wegmarken*. 1976. Edited by Friedrich-Wilhelm von Herrmann. *Pathmarks*. 1998. Edited by William McNeill. Cambridge: Cambridge University Press.

GA 15. *Seminare*. 1986. Edited by Curd Ochwadt. *Four Seminars*. 2003. Translated by Andrew Mitchell and François Raffoul. Bloomington: Indiana University Press. Martin Heidegger and Eugen Fink. *Heraclitus Seminar 1966/67*. 1993. Translated by Charles Seibert. Evanston, IL: Northwestern University Press.

GA 16. *Reden und andere Zeugnisse eines Lebensweges*. 2000. Edited by Hermann Heidegger. Memorial Address.

GA 24. *Die Grundprobleme der Phänomenologie*. 1975. Edited by Friedrich-Wilhelm von Herrmann. *Basic Problems of Phenomenology*. 1982. Translated by Albert Hofstadter. Bloomington: Indiana University Press.

GA 39. *Hölderlins Hymnen "Germanien" und "Der Rhein."* 1980. Edited by Susanne Ziegler. *Hölderlin's Hymns "Germania" and "The Rhine."* 2014. Translated by William McNeill and Julia Ireland. Bloomington: Indiana University Press.

GA 40. *Einführung in die Metaphysik.* 1983. Edited by Petra Jaeger. *Introduction to Metaphysics.* 2000. Translated by Gregory Fried and Richard Polt. New Haven, CT: Yale University Press.

GA 45. *Grundfragen der Philosophie: Ausgewählte "Probleme" der "Logik."* 1984. Edited by Friedrich-Wilhelm von Herrmann. *Basic Questions of Philosophy: Selected "Problems" of "Logic."* 1994. Translated by Richard Rojcewicz and Andre Schuwer. Bloomington: Indiana University Press.

GA 52. *Hölderlins Hymne "Andenken."* 1982. Edited by Curd Ochwadt. *Hölderlin's Hymn "Remembrance."* 2018. Translated by William McNeill and Julia Ireland. Bloomington: Indiana University Press.

GA 53. *Hölderlins Hymne "Der Ister."* 1984. Edited by Walter Biemel. *Hölderlin's Hymn "The Ister."* 1996. Translated by William McNeill and Julia Davis. Bloomington: Indiana University Press.

GA 55. *Heraklit: Der Anfang des abendländischen Denkens. Logik: Heraklits Lehre vom Logos.* 1979. Edited by Manfred S. Frings. *Heraclitus: The Inception of Occidental Thinking and Logic: Heraclitus' Doctrine of the Logos.* 2018. Translated by J. Goesser Assaiante and S. Montgomery Ewegen. London: Bloomsbury.

GA 65. *Beiträge zur Philosophie (vom Ereignis).* 1989. Edited by Friedrich-Wilhelm von Herrmann. *Contributions to Philosophy (of the Event).* 2012. Translated by Richard Rojcewicz and Daniela Vallega-Neu. Bloomington: Indiana University Press.

GA 66. *Besinnung.* 1997. Edited by Friedrich-Wilhelm von Herrmann. *Mindfulness.* 2006. Translated by Parvis Emad and Thomas Kalary. London: Continuum.

GA 69. *Die Geschichte des Seyns.* 1998. Edited by Peter Trawny. *The History of Beyng.* 2015. Translated by William McNeill and Jeffrey Powell. Bloomington: Indiana University Press.

GA 71. *Das Ereignis.* 2009. Edited by Friedrich-Wilhelm von Herrmann. *The Event.* 2013. Translated by Richard Rojcewicz. Bloomington: Indiana University Press.

GA 75. *Zu Hölderlin: Griechenlandreisen.* 2000. Edited by Curd Ochwadt.

GA 79. *Bremer und Freiburger Vorträge.* 1994. Edited by Petra Jaeger. *Bremen and Freiburg Lectures: "Insight into That Which Is" and "Basic Principles of Thinking."* 2012. Translated by Andrew J. Mitchell. Bloomington: Indiana University Press.

GA 81. *Gedachtes*. 2007. Edited by Paola-Ludovika Coriando. *Thought Poems*. 2012. Translated by Eoghan Walls. Lanham, MD: Rowman and Littlefield.

GA 82. *Zu eigenen Veröffentlichungen*. 2018. Edited by Friedrich-Wilhelm von Herrmann.

GA 89. *Zollikoner Seminare*. 2017. Edited by Peter Trawny. *Zollikon Seminars*. 2001. Translated by Franz Mayr and Richard Aksay. Evanston, IL: Northwestern University Press.

GA 94. *Überlegungen II–VI*. 2014. Edited by Peter Trawny. *Ponderings II–VI: Black Notebooks 1931–1938*. 2016. Translated by Richard Rojcewicz. Bloomington: Indiana University Press.

GA 96. *Überlegungen XII–XV*. 2014. Edited by Peter Trawny. *Ponderings XII–XV: Black Notebooks 1939–1941*. 2017. Translated by Richard Rojcewicz. Bloomington: Indiana University Press.

GA 97. *Anmerkungen II–V.* 2015. Edited by Peter Trawny.

GA 99. *Vier Hefte I und II*. 2019. Edited by Peter Trawny.

Other Texts Cited

Bambach, Charles. (2021). Sojourn. In Wrathall, Mark (ed.), *The Cambridge Heidegger Lexicon*. Oxford: Cambridge University Press, 685–689.

  (2022). *Of an Alien Homecoming*. New York: State University of New York Press.

Biemel, Walter, and Emad, Parvis. (1980). The Development of Heidegger's Concept of the Thing. *Southwestern Journal of Philosophy* 11(3), 47–66.

Capobianco, Richard. (2010). *Engaging Heidegger*. London: University of Toronto Press.

Capobianco, Richard. (2022). *Heidegger's Being: The Shimmering Unfolding*. London: University of Toronto Press.

Ewegen, S. Montgomery. (2021). Fighting Fire with Fire: Thinking Φύσις at the Inception. *Research in Phenomenology* 51(3), 414–425.

Gadamer, Hans-Georg. (1994). *Heidegger's Ways*. New York: University of New York Press.

Gosetti-Ferencei, Jennifer. (2004). *Heidegger, Hölderlin, and the Subject of Poetic Language*. New York: Fordham University Press.

Hatab, Lawrence. (2021). Language. In Wrathall, Mark (ed.), *The Cambridge Heidegger Lexicon*. Cambridge: Cambridge University Press, 447–453.

Hoy, David. (2008). The Politics of Temporality: Heidegger, Bourdieu, Benjamin, Derrida. In T. Miller (ed.), *Given World and Time: Temporalities in Context*. New York: CEU Press. 261–276.

References

Hyland, Drew. (1997). Caring for Myth: Heidegger, Plato, and the Myth of Cura. *Research in Phenomenology* 27(1), 90–102.
Irigaray, Luce. (1999). *The Forgetting of Air in Martin Heidegger*. Translated by Mary Beth Mader. London: Athlone Press.
Keiling, Tobias. (2021). Human Being. In Wrathall, Mark (ed.), *The Cambridge Heidegger Lexicon*. Cambridge: Cambridge University Press, 402–403.
Miller, James. (1996). Heidegger's Guilt. *Salimagundi* 109/110, 178–243.
Mitchell, Andrew. (2015). *The Fourfold: Reading the Late Heidegger*. Evanston, IL: Northwestern University Press.
Murray, Michael. (1980). Heidegger Hermeneutic Reading of Hölderlin: The Signs of the Time. *The Eighteenth Century* 21(1), 41–66.
Polt, Richard. (1999). *Heidegger: An Introduction*. Ithaca, NY: Cornell University Press.
  (2006). *The Emergency of Being: On Heidegger's "Contributions to Philosophy."* Ithaca, NY: Cornell University Press.
  (2020). A Running Leap into the There: Heidegger's "Running Notes on Being and Time." *Graduate Faculty Philosophy Journal* 41(1), 55–71.
Plato. (1997). *Protagoras*. Translated by Stanley Lombardo and Karen Bell. In *Plato's Complete Writings*. Edited by John Cooper. Indianapolis, IN: Hackett.
Richardson, William. (2003). *Heidegger: Through Phenomenology to Thought*. New York: Fordham University Press.
Sallis, John. (1980). Doubles of Anaximenes. In Jacobs, David (ed.), *The Presocratics after Heidegger*. New York: State University of New York Press, 145–152.
  (2000). *Force of Imagination*. Bloomington: Indiana University Press.
Savage, Robert. (2008). *Hölderlin after the Catastrophe: Heidegger, Adorno, Brecht*. Boydell & Brewer, Camden House.
Stiegler, Bernard (1998). *Technics and Time*. Stanford, CA: Stanford University Press.
Vallega-Neu, Daniela. (2003). *Heidegger's Contributions to Philosophy: An Introduction*. Bloomington: Indiana University Press.
  (2018). *Heidegger's Poietic Writings: From* Contributions to Philosophy *to* The Event. Bloomington: Indiana University Press.
Warminski, Andrzej. (1990). Monstrous History: Heidegger Reading Hölderlin. *Yale French Studies* 77, 193–209.
Winkler, Rafael. (2017). Dwelling and Hospitality. *Research in Phenomenology* 47(3), 366–387.
Withy, Katherine. (2021). "Uncanny." In Wrathall, Mark (ed.), *The Cambridge Heidegger Lexicon*. Oxford: Cambridge University Press, 789–791.

Cambridge Elements

The Philosophy of Martin Heidegger

Series Editors
Filippo Casati
Lehigh University

Filippo Casati is an Assistant Professor at Lehigh University. He has published an array of articles in such venues as The British Journal for the History of Philosophy, Synthese, Logic et Analyse, Philosophia, Philosophy Compass and The European Journal of Philosophy. He is the author of Heidegger and the Contradiction of Being (Routledge) and, with Daniel O. Dahlstrom, he edited Heidegger on logic (Cambridge University Press).

Daniel O. Dahlstrom
Boston University

Daniel O. Dahlstrom, John R. Silber Professor of Philosophy at Boston University, has edited twenty volumes, translated Mendelssohn, Schiller, Hegel, Husserl, Heidegger, and Landmann-Kalischer, and authored Heidegger's Concept of Truth (2001), The Heidegger Dictionary (2013; second extensively expanded edition, 2023), Identity, Authenticity, and Humility (2017) and over 185 essays, principally on 18th-20th century German philosophy. With Filippo Casati, he edited Heidegger on Logic (Cambridge University Press).

About the Series

A continual source of inspiration and controversy, the work of Martin Heidegger challenges thinkers across traditions and has opened up previously unexplored dimensions of Western thinking. The Elements in this series critically examine the continuing impact and promise of a thinker who transformed early twentieth-century phenomenology, spawned existentialism, gave new life to hermeneutics, celebrated the truthfulness of art and poetry, uncovered the hidden meaning of language and being, warned of "forgetting" being, and exposed the ominously deep roots of the essence of modern technology in Western metaphysics. Concise and structured overviews of Heidegger's philosophy offer original and clarifying approaches to the major themes of Heidegger's work, with fresh and provocative perspectives on its significance for contemporary thinking and existence.

Cambridge Elements ≡

The Philosophy of Martin Heidegger

Elements in the Series

Heidegger on Being Affected
Katherine Withy

Heidegger on Eastern/Asian Thought
Lin Ma

Heidegger on Thinking
Lee Braver

Heidegger's Concept of Science
Paul Goldberg

Heidegger on Poetic Thinking
Charles Bambach

Heidegger on Religion
Benjamin D. Crowe

Heidegger and Kierkegaard
George Pattison

Heidegger on Technology's Danger and Promise in the Age of AI
Iain D. Thomson

Heidegger On Presence
Richard Polt

Heidegger and the Elements of (Human) Being
S. Montgomery Ewegen

A full series listing is available at: www.cambridge.org/EPMH

For EU product safety concerns, contact us at Calle de José Abascal, 56–1°, 28003 Madrid, Spain or eugpsr@cambridge.org.

www.ingramcontent.com/pod-product-compliance
Ingram Content Group UK Ltd.
Pitfield, Milton Keynes, MK11 3LW, UK
UKHW030806150425
457293UK00016B/212